CULTURAL TRADITIONS IN NORTHERN IRELAND

ACKNOWLEDGEMENT

The Cultural Traditions Group is extremely grateful to the American Ireland Fund for their sponsorship of the lecture by Dr Roy Foster, and this publication of the conference proceedings.

Cultural Traditions in Northern Ireland

Inaugural lecture by Roy F. Foster

'Varieties of Irishness'

and

Proceedings of the Cultural Traditions Group Conference, 3–4, March 1989

Edited by Maurna Crozier

Institute of Irish Studies
The Queen's University of Belfast

Drawings in the text of Mourne country are the work of E. Estyn Evans. The cover illustration, 'Mossvale', is by John Luke.

First published 1989
by the Institute of Irish Studies
The Queen's University of Belfast
University Road, Belfast

ISBN 0 85389 328 4

Printed by W. & G. Baird Ltd, Antrim

CONTENTS

CULTURAL TRADITIONS GROUP

James Hawthorne, Chairman, Former Controller, BBC Northern Ireland.
Ronald Buchanan, Director, Institute of Irish Studies, Queen's University, Belfast.

Ian Adamson, Publisher and Farset Community Project, Belfast.
Paul Arthur, Senior Lecturer in Politics, University of Ulster.
Roger Blaney, Community Medicine.
Maurna Crozier, Research Fellow, Institute of Irish Studies, Queen's University, Belfast.
John Darby, Professor, Centre of Conflict Studies, University of Ulster.
Alan Gailey, Director, Ulster Folk and Transport Museum.
David Harkness, Professor of Irish History, Queen's University, Belfast.
Maurice Hayes, Ombudsman.
Peter Holmes, Department of Education.
Michael Longley, Arts Director, Arts Council of Northern Ireland.
Patrick Loughrey, Head of Educational Broadcasting, BBC Northern Ireland.
Jack Magee, President of the Linen Hall Library.
Tony McCusker, Central Community Relations Unit.
John Nolan, Director, Ulster Museum.
Ronnie Spence, Central Community Relations Unit.
Anne Tannahill, Publisher, Blackstaff Press.

PREFACE

Last autumn a number of people in education, the arts and communications were drawn together by the Central Community Relations Unit to explore ways of promoting a better understanding of, and a more constructive debate about, our different cultural traditions in Northern Ireland. Those exploratory discussions resulted in the formation of the Cultural Traditions Group operating under the aegis of the Institute of Irish Studies at Queen's University.

Such was the breadth of interest and experience of the members that there was some initial difficulty in putting past failures and disappointments aside and in arguing a case that, after more than twenty years of strife in Northern Ireland, fresh initiatives might in fact be possible. Through a process of self-searching debate, finely balanced at times between hope and cynicism, we agreed that not only might it be possible to make progress but also that we must seize present opportunities. Government is addressing community and cultural matters afresh. Radical changes in school curricula are being worked out. There is growing interest in local history, in communication through drama, through video and 'desk-top' technology. In spite of difficulties, the arts thrive. Publishing flourishes. Museums and libraries, large and small, are active and innovative and within mass media there are those who will support and publicise new ideas. Add to all this a promise of increased resources, coupled with a willingness to use them in a more effective and co-ordinated way, and we felt that we had, at the very least, a starting point.

Community relations and cultural diversity cannot be separated. While the first is a problem, the second is surely an asset, provided its richness can be celebrated in non-threatening ways. There is much in common across the so-called 'community divide' but what remains separate is of value also. There are many colours in our cultural spectrum, not just two.

The first endeavour of the Cultural Traditions Group has been to take some strides in 1989 to bring the recognition of cultural diversity more into the open. With this aim the Group organised a conference, launched with a public lecture, 'Varieties of Irishness' by Dr Roy Foster. On the following day the one hundred and forty delegates were addressed, briefly, by four speakers with different perspectives. Most time, however, was spent debating the issues of cultural diversity in seminars with the specific objective of making recommendations to key policy makers. This was the basic purpose of the conference on which the following pages report.

Numbers had to be restricted for practical reasons. The proceedings may not therefore represent as broad a span of experience and knowledge as we know exists. And many who attended were, inevitably, unable to catch the Speaker's eye during the plenary sessions. The conference was, however, only the start of a process of debate and discussion which, we hope, will extend more widely into all parts of the community.

Our special thanks are due to Dr Roy Foster for a memorable, scholarly and significant lecture; and to Dr George Quigley who, as Conference Chairman, conducted the proceedings with great warmth and authority.

JAMES HAWTHORNE
Chairman, Cultural Traditions Group

PART I

INAUGURAL LECTURE

'VARIETIES OF IRISHNESS'

by

Roy F. Foster

Conference Chairman's Introduction

George Quigley

Distinguished Guests:

Dr James Hawthorne's Cultural Traditions Group, working in conjunction with the Institute of Irish Studies at Queen's and the Government's Central Community Relations Unit, are to be warmly congratulated on their initiative in devising and organising this conference and for inaugurating it with this lecture. The Government has kindly provided funding for the conference. But special thanks are owed to the American Ireland Fund, which is sponsoring this lecture and the subsequent publication not only of the lecture but of the conference proceedings. Gratitude is also due to the University of Ulster for allowing these fine facilities to be used this afternoon.

It is highly appropriate that a Cultural Traditions Conference should be launched with a lecture by an historian of Dr Foster's eminence. Dwell on the past, says the old Russian proverb, and you'll lose one eye; ignore the past and you'll lose both eyes. Whether we like it or not, the past forms a kind of extended family. For some, the past is less friendly. Ghosts, as Ezra Pound said, move about, patched with histories. Derek Mahon, in his poem, 'As it should be', imagines the spectre of Irish history hunted down and shot, and looks forward to a more methodical world. And in William Faulkner's *The sound and the fury*, Questin Compson twists off the hands of the watch inherited from his grandfather, a general on the Southern side in the American Civil War. The watch symbolised the transmission of failure and defeat and the burden of remembering a past that paralyzes the present. But what seems like compulsive fate can be transformed, through narration, into the mastery of time. The historian who does it well has the privilege of breaking what Nietzsche called 'times's covetousness'.

The past fifty years in Ireland have seen an increasingly luxuriant flowering of the tree of historical knowledge. Gone are the inquiries into the past which were flawed by misplaced piety and loose rhetoric. These were not, of course, peculiarly Irish phenomena. The American historian Vann Woodward had cause to castigate the purposeful past of the rationalisers, the justifiers and the propagandists in his own country. The new historians are careful to show the contingent nature of history. As the natural scientist, Stephen Jay Gould, put it: 'Divert the comet, preserve the dinosaurs, and humans never evolve'. No law of nature decrees any particular evolutionary pathway. Blocked in one direction, history cascades down a different channel. The great merit of the historian, therefore, is to show us the choices which faced our predecessors, the limitations which constrained their freedom of choice, and why they chose as they did. He can help us to avoid the trap of seeing the past as a substance changeless and eternal, with a plan for the future contained in the beginning. Otherwise tradition is elevated over history. To become aware of time is to establish a more nuanced and qualified connection to the past, nourished but not bound by it (to adapt a phrase of Matthew Arnold).

In Hannah Arendt's vivid words, the true historian is mindful that Homer sang the deeds of the Trojans no less than those of the Achaeans and praised the glory of Hector no less than the greatness of Achilles. As she has also put it, 'true impartiality discards the alternative of victory and defeat, which moderns have felt expresses the "objective" judgment of history.' The true historian eschews the oversimplified antitheses and polarities which inevitably caricature and distort. The historian is, in fact, close to those natural scientists who, in the words of Freeman J. Dyson, consider the primal characteristics of life to be diversity rather than uniformity, the flexibility of the cell rather than the tyranny of the gene, the error tolerance of the whole rather than the precision of the parts.

Our distinguished guest lecturer today exemplifies in supreme fashion all that is best in the school of modern Irish historiography but he must also now rank as a major figure on the international scene. To seduce him from his work on the biography of Yeats to prepare and deliver this lecture was a triumph on the part of the organisers of the Conference. And how ironic that there should be entrusted to an historian the biography of a man who was attacked in his lifetime for his ignorance of history and who, as Professor Malcolm Brown has it, preferred to regard truth as the passionate conviction of just such a person as himself.

Dr Foster, who teaches at the University of London but is

currently at the Institute for Advanced Study at Princeton, is probably best known for his biographical studies of Parnell and Lord Randolph Churchill and, of course, for his recent *Modern Ireland*. Coming after a period which has seen a proliferation of specialist and thematic studies, he has provided the essential connective tissue. But, much more than that, he has recast the history of the period in a new perspective, preferring luminous to voluminous detail and demonstrating that adroit selection is in itself a significant analytical tool.

There is no question for him of substituting the studious monotone for the friction of argument. The words used recently of a book by the French historian, Le Goff, could equally be applied to Dr Foster's *Modern Ireland*: 'comparisons, metaphors, hypotheses leap from every page like so many startled hares' – except that in Dr Foster's case they are not all that startled! Take his reference to Anglo-Ireland in the eighteenth century. After talking about the correspondence of the great ladies he goes on: 'It is important to recapture a more gamy flavour – an echo of colonial Virginia, or even the Kenya highlands in the 1920's.'[1] Or his description of the marginalised Catholic country gentleman of the same period, about one of whom (Charles O'Conor of Belanagare) he says: 'O'Conor is a symbolic figure in his determination to compile materials of an Irish history that would clarify events rather than fight old battles over again.'[2] And there is his ability to select the telling quotation, like this from Henry Flood: 'Nothing that is subtle and intricate can ever be the foundation of settlement and concord.' Dr Foster caps it with a comment which encapsulates precisely his own wit and style: 'Constitutional insecurity ruled out political imagination: another enduring theme in Anglo-Irish relations.'[3] With scholarly excellence and such treasures as these available, he would be a very foolish person who would say of Dr Foster's book, as Dr Johnson did of Congreve's novels, that he would sooner praise them than read them.

Dr Foster, it gives me great pleasure, on behalf of all of us here, to invite you to deliver your lecture – *Varieties of Irishness*.

NOTES

1. R. F. Foster *Modern Ireland 1600–1972 (Penguin Press, 1988)*, p. 169.
2. *Ibid.* p. 210.
3. *Ibid.* p. 254.

VARIETIES OF IRISHNESS

by

Roy F. Foster

I have called this talk 'Varieties of Irishness' which is, as some of you may know, the title of the prologue to my recent book, and in a sense its theme. But I don't intend to regurgitate ideas already written down; rather, what I'm offering is a series of reflections on cultural diversity in Ireland – its roots, its interpretations, its implications. I say 'Ireland' fully understanding that the theme of the conference is Northern Ireland. But as a historian I think the diversity here, while obviously stemming from events and traditions peculiar to the north-east, can be illuminated by considering the cultural diversity discernible in the island as a whole in the generation before independence, round the turn of the century. And that is where I'd like to begin.

Any such consideration has to be inspired by the mingled admiration and reservations aroused by Leland Lyons' tremendously influential book *Culture and anarchy in Ireland 1890–1939*, which began life as a series of lectures delivered at Oxford in the Hilary Term of 1978. I was in the audience, and was riveted throughout. I still remember the impact of their concluding words. Our Irish diversity, Lyons said:

> has been a diversity of ways of life which are deeply embedded in the past and of which the much-advertised political differences are but the outward and visible sign. This was the true anarchy that beset the country. During the period from the fall of Parnell to the death of Yeats, it was not primarily an anarchy of violence in the streets, of contempt for law and order such as to make the island, or any part of it, permanently ungovernable. It was rather an anarchy in the mind and in the heart, an anarchy which forbade not just unity of territories, but also 'unity of being', an anarchy that sprang from the collision within a small and intimate island of seemingly irreconcilable cultures, unable to live together or to live apart, caught inextricably in the web of their tragic history.

Out of Ireland have we come;
Great hatred, little room,
Maimed us at the start.[1]

The sardonic tone was not entirely new for Lyons, but the bleak
pessimism was. It also, in a sense, ran counter to the school of liberal,
synthesizing historiography which he had come to embody. The
lectures, published, went on to tremendous and deserved success. In
many respects, *Culture and anarchy* was Lyons' best book. But the doubts
I felt while listening, along with the exhilaration, have remained.

The premise of the lectures, and a phrase whose derivation Lyons
carefully examined, involved what was called 'The battle of two
civilisations' – crudely, an Anglo-Irish pluralist, essentially secular
culture arrayed against the heady resurgence of Gaelic, Catholic,
separatist values. (Lyons had in fact already discussed this opposition, under the same title, in a brilliant chapter of his *Ireland since the
Famine*). His development of the theme at once raised some questions. His chosen representatives of the Anglo-Irish culture, like
Horace Plunkett and George Russell, maybe expressed a certain
version of secularism, but hardly answered for the Irish Protestant
consciousness at large. (Lyons partly evaded this difficulty by
partitioning off Ulster into a chapter of its own). More seriously, I
wondered about the retrospective angle of his historical view. This
was particularly notable when he dealt with the ferment of ideas
unleashed in the very early 1900s: because I thought much of this far
more identifiable with conciliation between cultural traditions than
confrontation. Lyons admitted: 'Superficially, it seemed, as the
nineteenth century ended, that a new era was opening, an era of
constructive thinking and doing in which men and women of
different cultures might join in friendly collaboration'.[2] Anyone who
reads the journalism and literature of the period must agree. But, he
goes on to say, beneath this the old fissures remained and the battle
of the two civilisations was drawing up its lines, to culminate in the
real battle of 1916.

I feel that this runs the risk of reading the story backwards – over
the shoulder, in a sense, across the gulf created by the events of
1914–18. That brief period saw not only the span of the Great War,
but the shelving of Home Rule, the tacit acceptance of Ulster's
secession, the takeover of the Gaelic League by the IRB, the Easter
Rising and subsequent executions, the Irish Convention, the con-
scription crisis, and the Sinn Fein election victory. Lyons' view,

however, implies that the lines of development were laid out independently of all this. It is, in fact, the Yeatsian reading of the period since Parnell's death. 'A disillusioned and embittered Ireland turned from parliamentary politics; an event was conceived; and the race began, as I think, to be troubled by that event's long gestation.'[3]

I've written elsewhere about what I think is the fallacious reasoning behind this, and I will not repeat myself at length here.[4] But when Yeats and others pressed this argument, as they began doing early on, it was in order to state a larger thesis: the idea that cultural revivalism, in the Irish context, deterministically produced extremist politics, and set up a zero-sum game which eliminated all middle ground. Douglas Hyde and other 'non-political' brokers of the early Gaelic League innocently opened a Pandora's Box. This idea, incidentally, rather ignores the fact that *before* his adoption of the Gaelic League, Hyde *had* already gone through his extremist political phase, and come out the other side; his youthful Fenianism and Anglophobia, revealed by Dominic Daly,[5] had given way to what he (rightly) saw as the more mature politics of cultural autonomy. (The Gaelic League, he later remarked, was 'charming until it became powerful'). Whether or not Hyde was proved wrong, he certainly was no innocent.

Yeats, however, possessed what his wife recalled as an astounding ability to sense 'the way things would look to people later on', and his version of inevitability took hold. It's no coincidence that Lyons was immersed in Yeats while preparing his lectures on 'Culture and anarchy'; the dichotomy set up by his argument fits tightly into the Yeatsian scheme of things, and has a satisfying coherence and symmetry. But it is also over-determined and reductionist – always a danger with Yeats, whose over-compensation as a marginalised Irish Protestant often led him into rigid and declamatory attitudes (as well as down many other strange paths, which belong in another lecture).

I want to try and keep *this* lecture fairly free both of Yeats and of personal anecdotes. But it's relevant perhaps to recall the reaction at a Dublin dinner table last summer when I described Yeats as a marginalised Irish Protestant. 'You can't talk about Yeats like that!' retorted a fellow guest indignantly. *'He was as Irish as I am.'* This was a latter-day echo of D. P. Moran's conclusion round the turn of the century, that 'the Gael must be the element that absorbs'. Lyons had picked out this phrase, presenting it as the inevitable outcome of Gaelic cultural revivalism, culminating in political separatism. But it's worth remembering that elsewhere in the same text *(The phil-*

osophy of Irish Ireland), Moran was scathing about 'prating mock-rebels ..... whining on about England stealing our woollen industries some hundreds of years ago'; that he queried the idea that the spirit of nationality was eternal; and that he mocked the idea of military assault on England as pointless. 'All we can do, and it should be enough for us, is remain Irish in spite of her, and work out our destiny in the very many fields in which we are free to do so.'

Moran's paper, *The Leader*, also remarked: 'Perhaps the greatest of all difficulties which underlie the whole of what is known as the Irish Revival is the length of time we are obliged to go back before we arrive at any mode of life that may with truth be termed distinctively Irish'.[6] This now seems like the kind of realistic reflection we'd associate more with the sane and balanced enquiries of a modern scholar like Estyn Evans. It's worth noting, too, the moderation and lack of Anglophobia in Hyde's early Gaelic League manifestoes at the same period. Even without invoking Plunkett, Russell, Synge and Yeats, there are arguments for seeing cultural diversity at the turn of the century in terms which are *not* necessarily confron-tational; leaving aside what happened to Irish politics with the precipitation of crisis by unforeseen contingencies from 1912 on.

II

Why, then, the prevalence of the opposing view? Who were the brokers of the idea of *inevitable* confrontation? It is significant that, when looking back at the extraordinary upheavals of the early twentieth century, *both* 'sides' had their reasons for presenting the same historical argument. There were the survivors among those who had been cultural entrepreneurs in the pre-revolutionary period – notably Yeats, tracing 1916 back to the influence of *Cathleen ni Houlihan* rather than to the logic of Liberal pusillanimity over the UVF and (more importantly) the knee-jerk Fenian reaction to England's involvement in an external war. There was also Hyde, victim of a *putsch* on the Gaelic League committee in 1915, and anxious to assert the inevitability of politics driving out cultural revolution, as well as his own unwitting initiation of the process. There were the new generation of political irreconcilables, of the Ernie O'Malley stamp, who left their own literary testaments – though they, significantly had *not* been active in the cultural initia-tives of the 1890s and early 1900s. All this lent credence as well as potency to the next generation of Gaelic League and GAA chauvinists, defining cultural identity as a matter of negation and exclusiveness rather than an affirmation of pluralism. This often meant deliberately embracing illogic – what Moran had contemptuously called 'thinking from hand to mouth'. There's a good example in a reminiscence by the old Belfast republican, Denis McCullough:

> We lived in dreams always; we never enjoyed them. I dreamed of an Ireland that never existed and never would exist. I dreamt of the people of Ireland as a heroic people, a Gaelic people; I dreamt of Ireland as different from what I see now – *not that I think I was wrong in this* . . .[7]

These elements represented, in a sense, the winning side convincing themselves that their myopia had been vindicated by history. But the losers, in post-revolutionary terms, also had a vested interest in asserting the inevitability of cultural diversity producing political confrontation. Augustine Birrell is one example: as his memoirs more or less argue, what *could* Dublin Castle do to stop the Rising, with the inevitable rise of an oppositional Gaelic culture predicating a nationalist revolution? (This argument had the added advantage of giving Liberals like Birrell a chance to imply that the Tory initiatives of 'constructive Unionism' had been irrelevant and doomed from the start). But others among the losers also seized the same point. The middle-class Irish parliamentarians, rhetorically as well as electorally trumped by Sinn Fein in 1918, went along with the determinist version rather than analysing the way they lost control of the commanding political heights apparently gained by 1914. (Until very recently, historians have tended to follow them in this evasion). Looking back over the early years of the twentieth century, the work of the Recess Committee, the two million acres redistributed by the Congested Districts Board and the land acts, the creation of committees which could accommodate not only Redmond and Healy sitting together, but even Colonel Saunderson – all this seemed to weigh little in the scale. Nowadays those of us who are also looking for unspectacular but real steps, taken forward together, may be less easily impressed by that apparent logic.

What I would like to query is the view that cultural diversity *was* inevitably confrontational, and to look briefly at the nineteenth century background. The idea of a revived 'Irish culture', and an Irish-Gaelic identity, is in its modern form firmly rooted in nineteenth century developments – historiographical, antiquarian, archaeological, as well as political and polemical. As has often been pointed out, the moving spirits in this intellectual exploration were initially often Protestant Unionists. There are some obvious reasons for this, grounded on social advantage, university education, and the amount of free time available to members of the Established Church. But to see their researches into Gaelic Ireland as necessarily having the ultimate effect of sawing off the branch upon which they were sitting, is again rather a retrospective view. They had their own psychological identification with Ireland, which was not threatened by an interest and a pride in the evidently ancient origins of Irish settlement and Irish culture. 'Victorian Ireland' could be middle-class, English-speaking and non-separatist in its politics, but no less 'Irish' for that. Samuel Ferguson is the figure most often instanced here; but his friend and colleague on the *Dublin University Magazine*, Isaac Butt, might be taken as another example. Recent research into Butt's early writings and career [8] has brilliantly queried the idea that defending the Fenians in 1867 somehow converted Butt to his peculiar and (to some of us) sympathetic brand of nationalism. It is, in fact, a presumption that assumes the pure milk of the separatist tradition is the only sustenance that can produce an Irish nationalist worthy of the name. Actually, the preconditions of Butt's nation-alism were set long before, in the 'national' preoccupations of the *D.U.M.* cliques of the 1830s, stimulated by their impatience with the shortcomings and incompetence of the English government, and most of all by the experience of the mismanagement of the Famine (Butt was, after all, also a political economist who swam against the current of the day). David Thornley's supposedly definitive study of Butt assumes throughout that he was somehow destined to miss the nationalist boat; however well-meaning, his background left him stranded on the shore. I'd rather see him as someone with a Protestant, even Orange, pedigree who shared in and helped create a sense of Irishness that accepted historic English influence while claiming realistic autonomy, and required no apology for its creden-tials at all.

Gaelic sympathies, Celtic researches, irritation with many of the actions of English government, and Anglicised educations could all coexist, and often did, among the Irish Victorian middle-class intelligentsia. (Yeats, pioneer of Irish folklore and Celtic legends, was first influenced by Scott and Macaulay). The great antiquarian, George Petrie, was also to be the great artistic memorialist of the early nineteenth century Irish landscape, and he derived his highly personalised approach to his native countryside from Wordsworth.

The personification and highly-charged nature of the Irish response to the land of Ireland is, of course, a tradition in Gaelic literature too; and it can, poetically speaking, be used to express conflicting and aggressive claims to the land, as in the 'aisling' poetry, or in Seamus Heaney's *Act of Union*. But it does not *only* belong to that tradition. The Irish identification with the land, its unique appearance, its light and shade, also owes much to English-derived romanticism (a sensation which one paradoxically receives even through tests like Ernie O'Malley's lyrical descriptions of bivouacs in the Tipperary mountains in *On another man's wound*). It has inspired masterpieces by Lloyd Praeger and Estyn Evans. And this might indicate that such perceptions can be reconciling and unifying too. I remember Professor J. C. Beckett, in a keynote address for the first Conference of Irish Historians in Britain, talking about those who live outside Ireland, and recalling a meeting with a fellow Ulsterman, a student, on – I think – a long-distance bus journey in Canada. They talked, as he remembered, enthusiastically about *the Irish land*; the uniquely varied landscape of this province; and its super-charged quality of beauty. It never, as he thought afterwards, occurred to either of them to consider, let alone investigate, what background or which 'tradition' each came from. Though historic claims to 'the land' might have separated them *within* Ulster, when they went abroad their common identification with it acted as a uniting factor. I'm sure many of us have had a similar experience. It was a resonant story, and I've often thought of it since.

To indicate this is not, perhaps, to draw attention to so very much. But in a similar way, I think it's worth remembering that the very fact of inhabiting Ireland imposes its own common bonds, and that these coexist with different cultural, religious and even political traditions. It has been pointed out by Professor Buchanan that in most of the fundamental characteristics of day-to-day living, the 'settlers' of Ulster were quickly homogenized with the natives. Folk belief about deeply opposed ways of life are described by Buchanan as 'a homely mixture of learned fact and heard tradition', and should be queried.

In his homeland the Scottish Planter had a way of life little different from his Irish neighbour. They lived in similar houses, used similar tools and implements, and marked the changing seasons with the same festivals and customs. In no sense can their settlement among the Irish in Ulster be regarded as a confron-

tation between alien cultures, for the bonds developed during the
first millennium AD and sustained through the medieval period
provided a common basis in folklife.[9]

It is true, of course, that the religious and linguistic divisions of the
early modern and modern periods imposed new barriers. But even
modern surveys (the classic studies by Rosemary Harris and Richard Rose, as well as later surveys by Hickey and Whyte) show that
the supposedly diverse cultural and religious traditions are compat-
ible with similar value systems and social practices. And similarly,
the social sub-cultures of nineteenth century Ireland were subtler,
more flexible and more interwoven than used to be admitted. Men
like Samuel Ferguson, preaching pluralism (and a sort of embryonic
home rule) in 1834, believed that joint study of Irish origins and
Ireland's history would have a reconciliatory effect. The tragedy is
that he was wrong, and over the ensuing century the effect of
studying Irish history, mediated through contemporary political
preconceptions, tended to have exactly the opposite result.[10]

This, of course, is where the over-used conception of historiographical 'revisionism' comes in. In the last generation, pathbreaking
work like that of Theo Hoppen, Tom Garvin, Vincent Comerford,
David Fitzpatrick and many others has delineated a political map
far less neatly demarcated than the landlord-versus-tenant, orange-
versus-green patterns of the old textbooks (now adhered to only by
wishful-thinking English and American observers). But 'revisionism' may be the wrong term here, because contemporary fiction
indicated a similarly varied universe at the time: witness the surreal
view of Dublin's middle-class and Bohemian worlds after the Union
in forgotten novels by John Banim, Gerald Griffin, and even Isaac
Butt, or the surprisingly subtle social gradations and interconnec-
tions in Trollope's *The Kellys and the O'Kellys*, or the variations of rural
Galway Catholics in George Moore's *Drama in Muslin,* or the
anatomy of Protestant County Cork in Somerville and Ross's *The
Real Charlotte*. Can it be a coincidence that all these texts were
banished from the supposedly authentic canon of Irish literature by
the exclusivist version of Irish culture peddled by Daniel Corkery?
But their credentials as Irish literature have now been reasserted
and so must the Irishness of the kind of sub-cultures they portray.

If Irish historians and literary critics now realise the viability of
cultural diversity, their agenda remains (as Lyons indicated in
Culture and anarchy) the study of mentalities – not only those of the

separatist nationalist persuasion (where Tom Garvin has made a start), but the mind of Castle Catholicism also, and *a fortiori* that of Presbyterian Ulster. In the process, unexpected overlaps may appear, and definitions of 'nationalism' may have to be broadened and in the process made inclusive rather than exclusive.

At the same time, it is worth reconsidering recurrent characteristics in Irish nationalism as normally conceived, which impose their own patterns, and work against an acceptance of diversity. One might instance Thomas Davis' use of anti-materialism as a strategy of distiguishing 'Irish' against 'English' values, and asserting moral superiority thereby – a line later adopted by Yeats as well as by de Valera.[11] This vein of argument should be investigated; on the one hand, to describe Ireland in 1903 as 'a place where men plough and sow and reap, not a place where there are great wheels turning and great chimneys vomiting smoke', clearly indicated that Belfast did not enter into this vision of Ireland. On the other hand, there *is* an analogous anti-materialism in Ulster Protestant ideology, and one cliché that has now mercifully been despatched is the notion of the 'hard-headed Ulsterman' whose political orientation is supposedly dictated by the interests of this pocket. The woeful inadequacy of the wishful thinking behind such an analysis is beginning to come into focus. It is possible that in studying anti-materialism, and the religious habit of mind, as well as confessional and sectarian modes of social organisation, a certain unity behind our diversities of culture would become surprisingly apparent. (Whether the implications are very cheerful for the secularists among us is, of course, another matter).

III

This raises the question of the various forms of Protestant commitment to Irish identity. We are all used to the disingenuous litany of Protestant names invoked in the extremist nationalist tradition – Tone, Emmet, Mitchel, Parnell (the Parnell of 1890–91, of course), and Childers. It's an argument used *ad nauseam* by de Valera, and still adverted to. The implication triumphantly drawn from it is that present-day Protestants have, therefore, nothing to fear from Irish nationalism; which is hardly logical, since all the figures in the extremist-nationalist-Protestant pantheon reacting diametrically against the general Protestant background are important as devi-

ants, not as representatives of a latent syndrome. Those who argue
the case for platonic Protestant nationalism do not mention one of
the silent subjects of twentieth century history, tacitly ignored by
both sides for their own purposes: the victimisation, murder and
banishment of 'ordinary' Protestants (not landowners or British
Army figures) in places like Limerick and Cork, *after* the Treaty, in
1922.[12] Here, thinking from hand to mouth approaches selective
amnesia.

I should like, however, to note some other kinds of Protestant
identity that are unequivocally Irish. Lyons, for instance, describes
Colonel George O'Callaghan Westropp (one of the bizarre heroes
resurrected by David Fitzpatrick's *Politics and Irish life*) as 'an
Anglo-Irish type still too little noticed by historians – the man or
woman in whom love of place transcended divisions based on
origins, religion or politics'.[13] The same characteristic is striking
when one focuses on a family like the Yeatses. Their background and
ethos was invincibly clerical, professional, middle-class Irish Protestant. But all of them – John Butler Yeats, his daughters Lily and
Lolly, his sons Willie and Jack – were absolutely and unquestionably
certain of their Irishness. Politically, this co-existed with opinions
that ranged from unreconstructed Buttism in John Butler Yeats and
increasing ambivalence about Irish nationalism in W.B., to out-and-
out republicanism in Jack. Religiously, it was not inconsistent with
the robust suspicion of Catholic mores displayed in Lily's letters, a
note also found (more surprisingly) in her brother's correspondence
with Lady Gregory. But their ethos cannot be seen as objectively
British-Imperialist, though that is how Sinn Fein (past and present)
choose to define more or less every Irish Protestant. There was
nothing hyphenated about the Yeatses' Irishness, just as there was
nothing English about their accents. And even at his most preten-
tious, W. B. Yeats was never accused of wanting to appear *British*.

The Yeatses were an extraordinary family in terms of genius, but
unexceptional for their religion and class in terms of their instinctive
national identification. At the same time, they were never shy – or
bogus – about admitting that much in their cultural conditioning
came from English intellectual sources. (An equally self-confident
and well-educated American would have had no difficulty in making
a similar admission). It's possible that Yeats' reliance on the idea of
an *Anima Mundi*, a common repository of world memories to which
all mankind has potential access, was partly directed by his experience of a common cultural pool of identification in things Irish,

which united him not only with Davis, Mangan, Ferguson, but also
with Allingham and O'Leary: as broad a political spectrum as could
be wished but all, in terms of cultural identity, absolutely Irish and
all educated in, and expressing themselves through, cultural norms
heavily influenced by English literature and English thought.

This leads on to consideration of another disingenuous argument,
which must be clarified: the notion that 'we Irish' are more influenced by Europe than by England. It was briefly, for obvious
reasons, very popular in the Republic in the early 1970s, but has a
much longer pedigree. It is satirised gently (I think) in Brian Friel's
Translations, where the hedge schoolmaster tells the English sur-
veyor: 'Wordsworth? .... no. I'm afraid we're not familiar with
your literature, Lieutenant. We feel closer to the warm Mediter-
ranean. We tend to overlook your island.'[14]

This is grandiose self-delusion. But one can still be told, in all
seriousness, as I was last year, that the process whereby some
Leaving Certificate students are claiming EEC rights to apply to
British universities will be swamped by a flood of intellectual
emigration when they discover how much better off they will be at
colleges in France and Germany. This betrays a touching if hilarious
nostalgia for the days when Irish missionaries dominated Louvain
and Salamanca; but it bears no resemblance to the realities of the
cultural and educational profile in Irish schools. What it represents
(like the Scots emphasis on the Auld Alliance with France) is a desire
to grasp at any argument that might support the idea of intellectual
independence from a powerful and culturally aggressive neighbour –
at the expense of facing up to the more interesting reality of a
culturally diverse inheritance within the polity. In a sense, the
pan-Celtic sub-group within late nineteenth century Gaelic revivalism adapted the same wishful-thinking argument when it empha-
sised Irish links with Scotland, Wales and Brittany; Yeats in 1897
claimed Renan, Lammenais, Chateaubriand and Villiers de l'Isle
Adam as Bretons rather than Frenchmen, and William Morris as a
great Welshman.

All this is laudably ingenious, but fantastical. Tom Garvin has
written with characteristic percipience about cultural insecurity in
late nineteenth century Ireland as an 'emotion in disguise'. Extreme
and exclusivist attitudes were a compensatory reaction to contempt,
anti-Catholicism, and separation from the establishment; the educational system mobilised a class of the discontented, up to school-
teacher and minor civil servant level, who formed the avant-garde of

the alienated. 'They projected their personal quandaries on to the social system in general, typically in the form of a noisy and romantic anti-British nationalism constructed from a mixture of traditional elements and new radical ideologies coming in from outside Ireland.'[15] It sounds strikingly familiar (as it's perhaps meant to). But the idea of an Irish culture affected more by Europe than by Britain is as unrealistic as the late nineteenth century notion of a world of prelapsarian innocence surviving on the Western seaboard. Nor is the interaction of European influence with Irish nationalism, where it *does* occur, an automatically good thing. The anti-semitic ravings of Arthur Griffith's *United Irishman* in the early 1900s make chilling reading. ('The Three Evil Influences of the century are the Pirate, the Freemason and the Jew').[16] And these obsessions, like Maud Gonne's similar opinions, derived directly from the anti-Dreyfus campaign in France, to which Griffith was violently committed. J. J. O'Kelly and J. J. Walsh, other brokers of Gaelicism and Anglophobia, were more virulent anti-semites still. Nor can the influence of Germany on the careers of Frank Ryan or Francis Stuart be seen as a particularly encouraging precedent. A genuine Irish Europeanism, or European Irishness, is devoutly to be hoped for. But it cannot be achieved simply as an adroit diversionary reaction conditioned by atavistic Anglophobia. In that case, it must produce, yet again, a rancid and self-congratulatory form of nativism. This characteristic, mercifully moderated in the south, persists in certain areas of cultural propaganda in the north. It needs to be opened up to an acceptance of the mixed cultural polity which we have all inherited, and in which we are all situated.

IV

It is time, then, to return to the views posited by *Culture and anarchy*. Essentially a view from the disillusioned south, Lyons' text presents the outcome of variations in Irishness as, inevitably, a monolithic confrontation:

Political solutions are indeed urgently needed, but they will continue to be as unavailing in the future as in the past if they go on ignoring the essence of the Irish situation, which is the collision of a variety of cultures within an island whose very smallness makes their juxtaposition potentially, and often actually, lethal. Recent events in Northern Ireland have certainly shown us that two very different communities are at death-grips with each other, but the fact that this conflict is so often described in religious terms has still further confounded confusion, leaving many observers convinced that a people so inveterately addicted to its ancient, obscure quarrels is best left to its own murderous devices.[17]

Such a view has since become, in a sense, entrenched – partly because of the persuasive and authoritative nature of Lyons' writing, and his own great stature as a historian. His subsequent, more optimistic statement that the 'roots of difference' were at last beginning to be explored was, in a sense, sidelined. The bleak implication of *Culture and anarchy* was given further credence by the miseries of day-to-day politics, and day-to-day murder, in Ireland over the decade since Lyons first lectured at Oxford. There is also a thought-provoking paradox, in that the historiographical tradition, whence Lyons came, had for forty years been resolutely breaking down the barriers imposed by pious nationalism – which was of course all to the good. But another, implicitly contradictory characteristic of the historiographical revolution, with its deliberately even-handed determination to give all sides their due, was a corresponding softening of certain sharp edges, and a blunting of embarrassing disjunctions. In Ireland, political aspirations and social thought, for Protestants as well as Catholics, often derive from ethics, theology and emotion rather than from economics or politics. The sectarian conflict and confessional identification present in every walk of Irish life were underplayed by the Moody school (including Lyons' own *Ireland since the Famine*), perhaps because they were temperamentally distasteful.

One of the interesting things about *Culture and anarchy* was that it confronted this phenomenon, reassessed it, and extended it – possibly to excess. Lyons' roping off of Ulster into one chapter, which I've mentioned, is one symptom of this. So is his virtual ignoring of World War I as a necessary precondition for 1916 (and much else). So, perhaps, is his choice of the eccentric Standish O'Grady as an emblematically doomed figure of the Protestant Anglo-Irish attempt at rapprochement. (Here, again, Lyons' inspiration was Yeats). At the same time, Lyons under-rated the influence (and efforts) of less spectacular non-Catholic, non-separatist nationalists such as Hubert Oldham of the *Dublin University Review* – perhaps because he assumed their loss of influence after the polarisation of 1912–14 was inevitable. Similarly, he saw the Gaelic League early on as a nursery of political separatism: an interpretation which fitted certain cells within the organisation, like the celebrated Keating Branch in Parnell Square, but not true universally until a late stage of the game. In fact the Keating Branch, a coven of *emigré* Munstermen conspiring against their Dublin colleagues, were seen by fellow Leaguers as 'footpads'. In the end, the Gaelic League had to be forcibly taken over by the strategy of handing out proxy votes to non-Irish-speaking IRB men (50 in Dundalk alone). By 1913, Pearse was declaring 'I have come to the conclusion that the Gaelic League, as the Gaelic League, is a spent force; and I am glad of it'.[18]

In terms of allowing for cultural diversity, the League had initially enabled Protestants to be Irish without being Catholic or separatist, and to annoy English speaking Catholic Irishmen by being more 'Irish' than they. And this particular vision was another casualty of political polarisation after 1912. But whether this was inevitable from the 1890s is a very different question. Similarly, Lyons' treatment, makes little of Hyde's development, and his increasing political moderation: except as yet another Irish Protestant inevitably retreating into the laager after playing with nationalist fire. And this is, I think, a misinterpretation.

There is also the question of the brilliantly entertaining but highly selective range of sources from which Lyons intuited Catholic and Protestant mentalities. Father Timothy Corcoran and the *Catholic Bulletin* may not have expressed the whole Catholic view; and at the same time, George Russell and the *Irish Statesman* represent a pretty idealised version of the Irish Protestant mind.[19] Lyons' last work was innovative, elegant, and deeply exciting; what its influence should now be doing is sending other scholars in a similar direction of cultural exploration, but casting their nets more widely.

And, if one dare say it, more speculatively and more optimistically. If A. T. Q. Stewart's belief that to the Irish all history is applied history is true, maybe it can be 'applied' to break down old ideas instead of reasserting old prejudices. If there's one single unalloyed good that has come out of the overdone debates about historical 'revisionism', it's the idea of the historian as subversive. We should be seeking out the interactions, paradoxes and sub-cultures – not only Oldham, with his *Dublin University Review* and his Contemporary Club bringing in Theosophists, Fenians and Trinity dons, but also speculative theories of origins (like Ian Adamson's), if only to rearrange the pieces in more surprising patterns. A new history could show that varieties of Irishness can be complementary rather than competing. Another key quote from Lyons:

Perhaps the most important consequence of the 1921 settlement was that by concentrating attention on physical boundaries and questions of political soveriegnty, it postponed almost till our own day any serious consideration of the cultural differences that underlay the partition of the country.

Elsewhere, though, he pessimistically remarked: 'the old argument for cultural fusion [revived by AE in the *Irish Statesman* during the 1920s] as usual went unregarded save by the few who were already converted'.[20] The implication is that this was as true for the 1970s as for half a century earlier. But there are alternatives to 'fusion' which need not necessarily be confrontation.

Perhaps, in the 1980s, it is time to investigate definitions of nationalism that could be inclusive rather than exclusive. I've talked of how, round 1900, an inclusive, energetic cultural debate was opening up between brokers of the different cultural traditions in Ireland – Plunkett, Griffith, Father Tom Finlay, Alice Milligan, Moore, O'Grady, Yeats, Synge, Moran. Reading their journals brings home the fact that they were not operating in several states of solipsistic isolation; they were engaging in dialogue with each other, however, angrily. Sometimes it seems that a similar process has been evolving in the columns of *Crane Bag, Fortnight,* the *Irish Review,* the Field Day pamphlets, *Krino,* the *New Nation, Alpha, Making Sense* – and this is only an off-the-cuff list of the proliferating publications noticed by a periodically returning emigrant. There is also the theatre of Friel, Parker, McGuinness, Murphy, Kilroy; and various initiatives on other levels from Belfast and Dublin. Along with this efflorescence there is, perhaps a Europeanisation which is less bogus than the kind I have already mentioned, and which may be able to teach us more.

It might, for instance, look at the political history of 'transfrontier' areas within the EEC – in which case, the supposed inroads made by the Hillsborough agreement into 'sovereignty' might look rather different. (In these areas, including regions like Alsace, Lichtenstein, and a *department* of the Pyrenees, external powers exercise authority on behalf of marooned minorities, through bipartisan commissions of governmental representatives of local and regional authorities of the countries concerned). The very notion of indivisible sovereignty is now being questioned;[21] feasible or not, the concepts of dual allegiance and cultural diversity are surely associated. Other areas where comparative historical study might open up new perspectives involve the practice of jurisdiction over designated individuals rather than specific territories: allegiance, in a sense, as an option rather than an imposition. Already it is being suggested that ethnic identification might be interpreted in a more flexible and contingent way, which might query the old zero-sum game, and break up some of the supposed congruences. We might even be beginning to question whether nationalism need imply the politics of old-fashioned separatist republicanism. (Especially since extremist Northern republicans are now faced with the prospect of a Southern state which no longer represents anything they want to 'unify' with, and will therefore have to be theoretically destabilised and reconstructed in its turn). A 'new nationalism', bearing in mind these subversive notions, might take many forms. Cultural self-confidence can exist without being yoked to a determinist and ideologically redundant notion of unilaterally-declared nation-statehood; political and cultural credentials have for too long been identified together. The slate of required qualifications for being Irish was beginning to be redefined a century ago, in the period Lyons wrote about; but the process was, in a sense, highjacked by a percussion of political upheavals. Might we not be coming back to a similar juncture now?

And as for cultural nationalism: need it be reactionary? Or exclusive? Or anti-modern? It is seen by many scholars as, historically, a defensive response to widespread social change, economic dislocation, and sectional decline; even as 'a disease of development'. But just as Unionism cannot continue to define itself only by negatives, an inclusive national ideal cannot look to Anglophobia as its cement, without becoming automatically negative. It is remarkable how long the inheritance of the turn-of-the-century formulations has lasted. The cultural roots of that nationalist revival stressed a perceived conflict between the values of the 'city' (English) and the 'country' (Irish). Despite a half-century of cultural imposition in independent Ireland, the values of the city may have won out. But that is no reason not to make 'the city' Irish too. Looking back once more to some unexpected aspects of turn-of-the-century nationalism, we find *The Leader* in 1901 defining the 'real Irish people' not as pampootie-wearing Aran fishermen, but as pettybourgeois artisans living in provincial towns in the south of

Ireland. Which is the beginning of realism; but the reference to the *south* of Ireland should be noted. It's significant that when analysing the revolutionary elite of the 1913–1922 period, Tom Garvin found a striking under-representation of Ulster – even of Catholic Ulster. One is reminded of an exchange in Stewart Parker's play *Northern Star*, where Henry Joy McCracken tells Jemmy Hope that Ireland is perceived by nationalists as 'a field with two men fighting over it, Cain and Abel. The bitterest fight in the history of man on this earth. We were city boys. What did we know about two men fighting over a field?' What official identity has lacked up to now is the sceptical perspective of the city boys.

And the need to modernise nationalism has tremendous relevance for cultural diversity and its acceptance in the north, as well as for a relaxation of attitudes in the south. Cannot a secular ethic now be taken as a reasonable aspiration in both parts of the island? With unconscious irony, Sean Cronin wrote a few years ago of how Pearse 'purified' Tone's politics of their irreligion. I sometimes feel we could do with some of that impurity again. It may have been apparent in the fact that the 'city' vote went against religious dictation in the recent referenda in the Republic. But we live with the results of the strategy whereby first Parnell in 1884–5, and then Sinn Fein in the First and Second Dail, made huge concessions to the Church in the field of education. It may have been in line with Irish historical precedent, but it utterly negated the pluralist, one nation rhetoric of official nationalism. If the idea that antagonistic attitudes and cultural apartness are sustained by separate schooling is a liberal cliche, it is a liberal cliche because it is true. One of the few unequivocally cheering pieces of news to come out of Ireland in recent weeks was a statement by those promoting integrated education that they have now eight flourishing schools and that they hope to be educating a third of the children of Northern Ireland by the year 2000. Cannot integrated education be presented, not as an anodyne and deracinating mish-mash, but as an affirmation of differences which might lead to mutual acceptance?

The question has been raised whether cultural nationalism, in the revival of the late nineteenth and early twentieth century, appealed to 'young religious and political intellectuals at times of national crisis, when the dominant ecclesiastical and political institutions of their society seemed powerless against an alien state'.[22] This seems, to a historian at least, unnecessarily schematic. But there may be grounds for hope that the discovery of an outward-looking and inclusive cultural nationalism, *not* predicated upon political and religious differences, will be the salient business of 'young' and not so young intellectuals and educators at this current crisis of both Irish states. If such a process, teamed with economic optimism, achieved its own momentum, specious hopes for 'political movement' might be left aside. More importantly, the hope of this lecture – that cultural diversity need not imply political confrontation – might get through to the rockface of attitudes in the housing estates of Belfast and Derry. Kevin Boyle and Tom Hadden have trenchantly pointed out that the simple solutions do not work.[23] If this means working on education at all levels, rather than politics, it may still be a step forward. And eventually, perhaps that is the kind of oxygen required to revive what Tom Paulin has caustically called the 'cadaver politic'. Here, too, the implicit 'cultural revolution' of attitudes which some observers have discerned in the south may be relevant.[24] To paraphrase a recent formulation, if a 'solution' is a political mirage, we should turn to irrigating the cultural and social desert.[25] It seems to me that our history contains encouraging signposts as well as depressing culs-de-sac, which is what I have tried to indicate this evening.

V

This has been rather a discursive talk, and I'm also very conscious of the impropriety of historians, southerners, emigrants, and especially a combination of all three, coming to Northern Ireland and talking airily about what goes on here. I've already mentioned the bitterly lamented Stewart Parker. There's a line in his play *Spokesong* about 'buzzards flocking in' to the North with notebooks and tape-recorders: to which should be added, lecture-notes. Still more, it may seem redundant to outline suggestions to an audience which includes so many people from whom I've learned anything I know about Ulster, its culture, its strengths and its flaws. But in this company, another name should be invoked – someone who, like Stewart Parker, is no longer with us and who, like Stewart, provided a voice Northern Ireland could ill afford to lose. I'm thinking of John Hewitt, who articulated that quintessential combination of Protestant scepticism and commitment, linked with a sense of place that was absolutely Irish. Hewitt's poetry tour with John Montague in 1970, 'The Planter and the Gael', was a landmark affirmation of creative cultural diversity. He once visualised himself as a Planter's Gothic church, like the one at Kilmore, with an ancient round tower encased inside, 'needled through every sentence I utter'.[26] Like his own tough-minded poetry, the image faced up to allegiances that might have been formally divided, but could be personally reconciled. It's a cautious ambition; but let's end this paper, and begin this conference, with that.

NOTES

1. F. S. L. Lyons, *Culture and anarchy in Ireland 1890–1939* (Oxford, 1979), p.177.
2. *Ibid*, p.54.
3. W. B. Yeats, *Autobiographies* (London, 1955), p.559.
4. See R. F. Foster, 'Anglo-Irish literature, Gaelic nationalism and Irish politics in the 1890s' in J. M. W. Bean (ed.), *The political culture of modern Britain: studies in memory of Stephen Koss* (London, 1987); also Foster, *Modern Ireland 1600–1972* (London, 1988).
5. Dominic Daly, *The young Douglas Hyde: The dawn of the Irish revolution and renaissance 1874–1893* (Dublin, 1974).
6. 6 February 1904.
7. Tom Garvin, *Nationalist revolutionaries in Ireland* (Oxford, 1988), p.xi.
8. This is one theme in an important Ph.D. thesis, 'The philosophy of Irish Toryism', currently being completed at the University of London by Joe A. Spence.
9. See F. W. Boal and J. N. H. Douglas (eds), *Integration and division: geographical perspectives on the Northern Ireland problem* (Belfast, 1982), p.67.
10. See R. F. Foster, 'History and the Irish Question', *Transactions of the Royal Historical Society* xxxiii (1983).
11. W. B. Yeats in New York, 1903; quoted in E. Cullingford, *Yeats, Ireland and Fascism* (London, 1981), p.25.
12. See Dennis Kennedy, *The widening gulf: Northern attitudes to the Independent Irish State 1919–49* (Belfast, 1988), ch.7.
13. *Culture and anarchy*, p.105.
14. Brian Friel. *Translations* (London, 1981), p.49 (Act II, scene 1).
15. *Nationalist Revolutionaries in Ireland*, pp 23, 46.
16. 23 September 1899.
17. *Culture and anarchy*, pp 1–2.
18. *An Claideamh Soluis*, 8 November 1913.
19. See M. O'Callaghan, 'Language, nationality and cultural identity in the Irish Free State 1922–27: the *Irish Statesman* and the *Catholic Bulletin* reappraised', *Irish Historical Studies* xxiv no 94 (November 1984).
20. *Culture and anarchy*, p.168.
21. See M. Dent, 'The feasibility of shared sovereignty (and shared authority)' in Charles Townshend (ed.), *Consensus in Ireland: approaches and recessions* (Oxford, 1988).
22. John Hutchinson, *The dynamics of cultural nationalism: The Gaelic Revival and the creation of the Irish nation state* (London, 1987), p.233.
23. K. Boyle and T. Hadden, *Ireland: a positive proposal* (Harmondsorth, 1985).

24. Tom Garvin in C. Townshend, *op. cit.*, p.103.
25. E. Moxon-Browne, *Nation, class and creed in Northern Ireland* (Aldershot, 1983), p.17.
26. Planter's Gothic: an essay in discursive autobiography' in Tom Clyde (ed.), *Ancestral voices: the selected prose of John Hewitt* (Belfast, 1987), p.9.

CHAIRMAN'S RESPONSE

May I thank you most warmly on behalf of all of us for a lecture which even exceeded our very high expectations.

It may disturb any – none of them, I am sure, in this audience – who prefer the vapid to the controversial. But it is precisely the purpose of a conference of this kind to stimulate and challenge. Your lecture, the product of evident sincerity and concern, has certainly done that. It has been said that Irish history, like the old-time religion, gives true baptism only through total immersion. For that we must go to your books. But if there be any here who have been unfamiliar with your work, the drops sprinkled on the forehead today presage a new harvest of Foster afficionados. A speaker once warned his audience that, if they thought his message was particularly clear, they had probably misunderstood what he had said. I am afraid that, judged by that criterion, you must have been grossly misunderstood today. But that other speaker was a mere economist. Your lecture was a model of clarity.

It also exemplified in high degree how, in Professor Terence Brown's words, modern Irish historians are exploring their country's past without palpable design upon their readers.[1] We have been shown the stubborn complexity of Irish reality, a compound of continuity and change. The multiple perspectives of the historian encourage us to be challenged rather than dismayed by the irreducible ambiguities which we have inherited. Viewed in this way, the study of history can, I suggest, be a major humanising influence. It can enable us to explore the basis of what the American historian Richard Hofstadter called 'comity' – the tolerant attitude which may seek the defeat of an opposing interest on matters of policy, but at the same time does not deny the legitimacy of its existence or values. Diversity need not lead to destructive antagonism nor need group identity detract from the integrity of community. To adapt the poet John Montague, history can prevent tradition becoming an anachronistic defence against experience. It may also enhance our capacity to accommodate contradiction.

I would ask all our distinguished guests to conclude these proceedings by renewing their thanks for what, Sir, was a magnificent lecture.

NOTE

1. T. Brown *A social and cultural history of Ireland 1922–1985* (Fontana, 1985).

PART II

ADDRESSES AND DISCUSSION

CHAIRMAN'S INTRODUCTION

I am sure you would wish me to congratulate warmly the Cultural Traditions Group for their initiative in conceiving, promoting and organising this event. I can claim no share of the credit for that. But I was honoured to be asked to chair the conference and very pleased to accept the invitation. I trust that it will be a successful conference, where all will feel able to speak freely, even where that involves the expression of a possibly unpopular opinion. As Arthur Koestler said, if the creator had a purpose in providing us with a neck, he surely meant us to stick it out – at least occasionally. The only requirement is obviously that our discussions should be of a kind which does not in itself increase disharmony.

It is right to recognise at the very beginning of today's proceedings that an immense amount of work has been done over many years in the field of culture retrieval, much of it by many of those attending the conference. We stand on their shoulders. But it is always useful to take stock, to see what lessons can be learnt from the work done to date, to consider how it might be reinforced and extended, and, above all, to explore ways of ensuring that the work makes maximum impact on the community. Many of those present here are well placed not just to chart the way forward but to make things happen. I am certain that we all want – and need – to give our proceedings a sharp cutting edge, both as regards analysis and projected outcome. Few topics lend themselves more to the spongy concept, the conceptual ambiguity or the amorphous term.

Before inviting our four speakers to launch the first session, I would like to make a few introductory observations and pose a few questions which I hope may be helpful by way of backcloth.

First of all, lest we be misinterpreted, I think it is important to acknowledge that nothing likely to emerge from this conference provides a complete answer to the problems by which Northern Ireland is beset. Theorists of organisation talk about the hard S's – things like strategies, structures and systems – and the soft S's – things like style and staff and skills. I believe that we belong here largely to the soft S's. We belong more to the poets who (like, say, a Robert Lowell) see it as their job to mend and reconnect and less to those whose function it is to mediate through the political process the arrangements conducive to normal living. But the soft S's are as indispensable in the community as in other types of organisation. The search for community is therefore a vital ingredient in a larger process.

In this connection it is worth recalling Seamus Heaney's statement that 'in this country, for a long while to come, a refinement of feelings will be more urgent than a reframing of policies and constitutions'.[1] Some have asked: 'their feelings about what subjects will refine the feelings of society?' Perhaps we might sharpen that question to read: can more knowledge and more understanding of the habitat, heritage and history which have shaped what Estyn Evans calls the 'personality of Ulster' contribute to that very necessary refinement of feelings? If so, precisely how?

When we talk about culture, do we mean more than matters of habitat, heritage and history, which illustrate the inevitable pluralism that results from thousands of years of varied human settlement? Do we accept the view that a culture is not just a collection of discrete institutions and traits but an integrated complex, more or less tightly organised around some central motif, some generalised attitude towards reality - that culture is, in fact, akin to an art-style? Have we examples in Northern Ireland of this phenonemon of cohesive cultural ethos, in which inherited values of all kinds (including religious values) cross-validate each other? What is the relevance of this, if any, to the way in which we approach our task? How relevant is it that the different strands of Irish life may be on the way to becoming 'wraiths of the past' (Professor Terence Brown's term) within the homogeneity of a consumer society?

How do we overcome the constraints imposed by the fact that so many people are organised in largely exclusive social networks, with mainly segregated education and much segregated housing? Do we distinguish between the rural and the urban situation?

What, if any, account do we need to take of recent theoretical work on how the social groups (to which we all need to belong) acquire their identity and sustain it – the suggestion that they exaggerate difference and, particularly when feeling threatened, assert superiority? One writer has suggested that the fostering of difference in fact constitutes the social construction of ethnicity. Do we want to *enhance* or *attenuate* ethnic identity?

How can it be prevented from becoming ethnocentric, an extreme form of group egotism whereby other groups – or often, in the Northern Ireland case, *the* other group - are scaled and rated with reference to our own?

Can it be taken as read that we desire a plural society, reflecting the diversity of our traditions, and that we eschew any attempt at contrived assimilation which weakens the internal solidarity of groups? But how does one at the same time achieve a *stable* pluralism, with enough conformity to a minimum of general norms to enable people to get along?

American experience is quite treacherous in this respect. It has been argued that 'cultural pluralism' in the United States was predicated upon, and made possible by, a high degree of consensus and that cultural pluralism was grounded on, and even consummated in, the American idea. In other words, the rhetoric of American identity - of the elect on their way to the New Jerusalem – supplied the spiritual cohesion which the secular pluralism demanded and provided a ready framework for acculturation. Thus the rhetoric of fusion at one and the same time reflected the triumph of an extraordinary cultural hegemony and also masked the acute fragmentation of American life. A formidable tribute indeed to the power of myth to shape perception and experience. Here, as elsewhere, I summarise a point of view, so far as is possible, in the words of its proponents.

It has been held that the primary fact about group life in any society is not that each has its own distinctive culture but the contact which the groups have with each other, and how they react to, and mutually influence, each other. What opportunities do they have to acquire the memories, sentiments and attitudes of other persons and groups and, by sharing their experience and history, become incorporated with them in a common cultural life? And I distinguish that 'common cultural life' from cultural integration.

To what extent do we in Northern Ireland have such interaction and how do we strengthen it, and what should its nature be? I now detect some scepticism about inter-group encounter which promotes contact but *avoids* confrontation of different attitudes and value positions and plays down difference. Consensus, it has been said, should not be the aim (of contact) but rather increased awareness, sensitivity and comprehension. Or, again, it has been pointed out that it is fairly easy to promote a knowledge of someone else's value position but to expect, or demand, acceptance (ie: of the right to exist of a value position alien to one's own) is another matter. Do we extrapolate too readily from what may promote tolerance at an *inter-personal* level but may prove somewhat ineffectual in terms of *inter-group* relations?

There seems to be broad recognition that distinctiveness – even separateness – need not be equivalent to divisiveness. Nor is it even the *perception* of the other group's distinctiveness which constitutes the difficulty. Instead (as I have seen it argued) it is the meanings which are attributed to the overt demonstrations of these cultural affiliations and the fact that these stand as public proclamations of the cultural aspirations of the group concerned, and are interpreted as being intended to cause offence.

The distinguished American historian, David M. Potter, has argued that cultural diversity is never the direct cause of conflict and that such diversity will generate friction only when it has been translated into opposing policies for dealing with particular questions which bear on the interests of the groups concerned. On this theory, the disruptive potential inherent in cultural diversity remains latent until conflicts of interest bring it into play. On the other hand it is comforting to note that between *diverse cultures* strong *community of interests* may develop and should clearly be fostered.

Let me emphasise that all these points do not necessarily require consideration during this conference. But it would be my view that it will be desirable for at least some of them to be addressed at some stage if whatever the result from our proceedings today is to play an effective role in enriching our society. By effective I mean achieving critical mass and permeating the whole society, not being confined to those already related in an informed and mature way to our cultural traditions.

Seamus Heaney has a phrase about dwelling without cultural anxiety amongst the usual landmarks of your life. And should we not add 'and amongst the landmarks of other lives which may be very different'?

I come now with great pleasure to the speakers who are to give four perspectives on the existence of distinctive cultural traditions in Northern Ireland and make suggestions.

Michael Longley

Poet, autobiographer, editor and expositor of MacNeice before it became fashionable to be so, and wordsmith of unforgettable lines and phrases:

> Mind open like a half-door
> To the speckled hill, the plover's shore.

We welcome the opportunity to look through the half door *into* Michael Longley this morning.

Jack Magee

It has been said of place names that they lie deep, like some script indelibly written into the nervous system. That could be expanded to apply to Jack Magee's sense of place and past. In his deft grasp, to take just one example, the records of the nineteenth century school inspectors shed a torch on far broader areas of Irish history. And his 1974 volume, *Crisis and Conflict*, shows his ability to paint on canvasses large and small.

Christopher Napier

Thomas Kinsella said: 'The Irish tradition is a matter of . . . two major bodies of poetry asking to be understood together as functions of a shared and painful history.' He went on to warn against missing the opportunity of responding to 'the oldest vernacular literature in Western Europe, as it survives a change of vernacular'.[2]

David Trimble

A man equally at home in the minutiae of housing law, in turbulent political waters, or reflecting at greater leisure on his heritage and its future. I suspect it is the latter which he will be doing this morning.

NOTES

1. S. Heaney (ed.) *Soundings* (Blackstaff Press, 1972).
2. T. Kinsella (ed.) *New Oxford Book of Irish Verses* (1986).

SPEAKERS

MICHAEL LONGLEY

At primary school (and later at grammar school) there was next to nothing on the curriculum to suggest that we were living on the island of Ireland and in the Province of Ulster: little or no Irish history except when it impinged on the grand parade of English monarchs; little or no Irish literature; no Irish art; no Irish music. When we sang in music classes we mouthed English songs. One inspector criticised our accents and forced us to sing 'Each with his bonny lawss, A-daucning on the grawss.' A great deal of our schoolboy mythology was concerned with Roman Catholics. Why did Taigs cross themselves? What dark practices lurked behind confession and Mass? Didn't the nuns kidnap little girls and imprison them behind the suspiciously high walls of the big convent at the top of the Ormeau Road? When ignorance and superstition replace curiosity and information the result is *fear*.

In the late Fifties and early Sixties when I attended Trinity College Dublin the two parts of Ireland were studiously incurious about each other. And it was the time of the Ban. The Catholic Church decreed that it was a mortal sin for Catholics to enroll at Trinity. I did become friendly with two Catholics – one an American and the other from Rhodesia! Not exactly The Real Thing! I didn't get to know The Real Thing until I returned to Belfast to teach. Poetry brought together a number of us in a way that denied sect and class. It now seems to me quite extraordinary that I was twenty-three before I could count Northern Irish Catholics among my close friends. This was when my education as an Ulsterman really began. And at this time I also began to discover 'the prophets' – John Hewitt, Estyn Evans, Michael J. Murphy, Lloyd Praegar, Louis MacNeice. The list could go on.

What I have been describing is an abnormality – the abnormality of cultural apartheid. It operates even more powerfully today; and it is sustained by both communities to their mutual impoverishment.

Ulstermen (and women) could be the beneficiaries of a unique cultural confluence which embraces the qualities of the Irish, the Scottish, the English and the Anglo/Irish. (As an aside I would like to remark that those who seek to describe or alter the relationship between the two islands tend to undervalue, even to ignore, the Scottish horizon, the Mull of Kintyre visible from the Glens of Antrim. Presbyterians used to row across the sea to worship in Scotland on Sundays. Ian Paisley may look and sound out of place in London; but in Glasgow he is perfectly comprehensible. In America they refer to the Scots-Irish – a usage which recognises the still partial nature of the sea change.)

Years ago the Ulster poet and erstwhile Presbyterian minister, W. R. Rodgers, wrote about 'the creative wave of self consciousness which occurs wherever two racial patterns meet'. By comparison the concepts of a purely Green Ireland and an Orange Ulster seem impoverished, especially since you cannot have one without the other. Nearly as unattractive would be a melding in which the colours run so wetly together that they dissolve into toneless uniformity. A witty little poem by John Hewitt sums up what I am trying to say:

Cultra Manor: The Ulster Folk Museum

After looking at the enlarged photographs
of obsolete rural crafts, the bearded man
winnowing, the women in long skirts
at their embroidery,
the objects on open display, the churn,
the snuff-mill, the dogskin float,
in the Manorhouse galleries,
we walked among the trees to the half dozen
re-erected workshops and cottages
transported from the edge of our region,
tidy and white in the mild April sun.

Passing between the archetypal round pillars
with the open five-barred gate,
my friend John said:
What they need now, somewhere about here
is a field for the faction fights.[1]

We are not talking about some wishy-washy middle ground. Culture – the arts – have no future in Ulster unless they venture into dangerous challenging areas. And Ulster will become a really unhealthy place unless it tries to accommodate the challenges. As one literary critic has put it, Ulster is culturally a corridor. 'The literature produced by Ulster people suggests that its inhabitants might accept this province-in-two-contexts as a cultural corridor. Unionists want to block the corridor at one end, republicans at the other. Culture, like common sense, insists it can't be done. Ulster Irishness and Ulster Britishness are bound to each other and to Ireland and to Britain. Only by promoting circulation within and through Ulster will the place ever be part of a healthy system.'[2]

I believe that the arts have a crucial role to play in promoting the health of this place. I have quoted elsewhere an analogy of Cyril Connolly's. He compares arts' relationship with the community to the influence on the body of certain glands. Small and seemingly unimportant they may be, but when they are removed, the body dies. The 'regional identity' which John Hewitt so desired, demands the involvement of artists in the community, an exchange of energies between the two. Again in Hewitt's words, 'out of that loyalty to our own place, rooted in honest history, in familiar folkways and know-ledge, phrased in our own dialect, there should emerge a culture and an attitude individual and distinctive, a fine contribution to the European inheritance and no mere echo of the thought and imagin-ation of another people or another land'.[3]

This conference would be worthwhile even if there was not a communal problem. It will have achieved something if young people from Ulster are exposed to the best that Ulster artists, especially writers, have produced. It will have achieved something if we convince our pro-consuls and policy-makers that culturally speaking we are sitting on a gold mine – and by culture I mean the story teller John Campbell and the singer Len Graham who entertained us last night, just as much as the Ulster Orchestra. Let us not forget that Ulster is one of the most culturally vibrant corners of Europe. The artist is uniquely qualified to demonstrate how both our cultures can define themselves by a profound and patient scrutiny of each other. In the words of the great English poet W. H. Auden:

> .... all real unity commences
> In consciousness of differences.[4]

NOTES

1. Alan Warner (ed.) *The Selected John Hewitt* (Blackstaff Press, 1981).
2. Edna Longley, *Fortnight* no 256, November, 1987.
3. John Hewitt, 'The Bitter Ground' *Ancestral Voices* (Belfast: Blackstaff Press, 1987).
4. W. H. Auden, *New Year Letter* (London: Faber and Faber).

JACK MAGEE

Some years ago Ulster Television transmitted a programme with the arresting title 'Irish history will be the death of us all'. As I remember it, the programme was an indictment of Irish history as popularly perceived, and claimed that, despite the revisions of modern scholars, each faction of our divided community in Northern Ireland still clung tenaciously to its traditional version of the past, with its different heroes, rituals and anniversaries. The consequence was that protestants and catholics, unionists and nationalists, had little common ground, and because of the circumstances in which their mythologies had been acquired, had no understanding of the historical basis of each other's grievances and fears. The programme concluded that Irish history was a damnable and divisive inheritance and an insuperable barrier to reconciliation and peace.

An exaggeration? Undoubtedly, but the indictment does contain an uncomfortable degree of truth. The new historiography, to which Dr Roy Foster referred in his lecture, has had limited impact on our schools and practically none at all on the public at large. The Irish, despite what outsiders believe, are not preoccupied with history but obsessed with divisive and largely sectarian mythologies acquired as part of their political or religious experience. Like it or not we have to live with the past; but to concentrate on grievance alone, and to project Irish history as a standing indictment of Britain is to create a Frankenstein monster which will destroy us all. Certainly we shall never move towards the concept of a shared identity here, if we cannot correct these versions of Irish history by the work we do in our schools. I must say, however, that I have some reservations about the ability of any educational system to modify attitudes and prejudices acquired early by children in their home environment; but if our people are to live in harmony here, our students must be given an opportunity to understand one another, and to appreciate the contribution which each group that has settled here has made to our common inheritance. For that reason I applaud the efforts which the Department of Education is making, through the cross-community contact scheme, through the Education for Mutual Understanding programme and through the panels recently appointed to monitor curriculum development, to do just that. My only regret is that the attempt was not made sooner. Some of you may recall that nearly twenty years ago, in a paper for an Irish Association Conference at Queen's University, Belfast, I outlined a programme of a somewhat similar nature to that being proposed today. I feared then – what has since become a reality – that the history being taught in some of our schools was so unbalanced as to excite emotions, and might in certain circumstances be used as the moral justification for taking life.

I advocated in 1970 – and still do – that in primary schools and the lower forms of secondary schools less political history and more social and economic history be taught. Violence has been a fact of life here over the centuries and Anglo-Irish relations have been far from happy; but to portray modern Irish history in terms of a single theme – the struggle for political independence – is a serious and dangerous distortion of reality. What I suggested was the shattering of the traditional moulds of Irish history so that new patterns might be formed and fresh interpretations emerge. Thus Celts, Vikings, Normans, Scots and English might be seen for what they actually were, successive waves of immigrants who inter-mingled and fused, and have each left their marks on our settlement patterns, our rural customs and traditions, our place-names and colloquial speech. This is very different from the traditional 'them' and 'us' versions of the Irish past which have prevented any kind of coherent community sense developing in the present. I was not advocating the flattening out of cultural differences, but rather the acceptance of cultural diversity in an atmosphere of tolerance.

Political differences, of course, cannot be ignored for that would leave our young people bereft of any understanding of current affairs. But they are not the whole of our history and I wonder whether their study could not be postponed until pupils are mature enough to be given a balanced treatment of them. Undertaken too early they consolidate prejudices acquired at home or in the community, and make it difficult for adolescents to take a dispassionate attitude to political questions. The current obsession with political history can be tackled by the inclusion of material from the fields of literature, the arts, science and technology as well as economics and folk life. Then the achievements of men like William Dargan, Thomas Andrews, Eugene O'Curry and John O'Donovan can be

measured against the achievements of O'Donovan Rossa and the
'Manchester Martyrs', and the grip of politics on Irish history will be
eased.

Such an approach will involve the use of a wide range of learning
materials as part of the curriculum, and a committee of the Cultural
Traditions Group will make recommendations on the matter. What
I would like to see are Protestant and Catholic teachers collaborat-
ing in the production of books, education packs and video tapes,
either as joint authors or on an editorial board. Co-operation of this
sort might not only eliminate prejudice, it might also ensure that the
cultural richness of practically every tradition would find a place,
'Orange' as well as 'Green'. We have in Northern Ireland the
authors and publishers to undertake such work, if financial support
was made available to them, particularly in the early years.

However, the great challenge to those of us seeking to promote
acceptance of cultural diversity is the wider community, the so-
called 'man in the street'. In his inaugural lecture at Queen's
University Professor Harkness recognised that challenge. 'Only the
adult community,' he said, 'can break the vicious circle of prejudice
and myth that is preventing the schools from creating a new
generation, free of partial, limited and warped understanding.'
Breaking the vicious circle is not going to be easy. The media
(particularly radio and television), the extra-mural departments of
our universities, the Worker's Education Association and the trade
unions have a positive contribution to make here. But one of the most
hopeful developments of recent years has been the spontaneous
growth of local history and heritage societies. In their membership
they transcend barriers of religion, politics and class, and find
common ground in the locality or county whose past is their concern.
With no financial resources except those raised by or from their
members, they organize lectures, exhibitions and field trips, and in
recent years many have begun to publish journals. These latter are of
variable quality, but the best of them attract contributions which
have raised local studies from the little esteemed pastime of antiqua-
rians to one more nearly of parity with national history. Nowadays
articles by the foremost authorities in their fields may be found in
journals such as *The Clogher Record, The Glynns,* and *Seanch as Ard Mhacha.*

Enhanced status has brought increased influence, and the societies have achieved a collective voice through the Federation of
Ulster Local Studies. In 1980 the Federation articulated the philosophy which motivated its activities:

Local studies draw people together to seek understanding rather than self-justification; to find their history and their shared community. Local studies are involved with identity, with community, with understanding, and as such are a civilising influence on any country.

If our aim is to promote contact between people of different backgrounds and to encourage a constructive debate on our environmental and historical heritage, the local history societies provide ready-made forums. In my opinion they are the greatest integrating force in Northern Ireland today, and as such deserve recognition and support.

The Federation for Local Studies has for some years been creating a Trust Fund, the income from which will be used to assist with local history publications, and the development of links between organisations which promote shared interests throughout the province. This is the sort of enterprise the Cultural Traditions Group should encourage and a grant to the Trust Fund would give a worth-while return in terms of community relations.

Local studies owe much of their success to the help they receive from the museums, the regional ones at Armagh, Enniskillen and Downpatrick, as well as the two national museums in Belfast. Nor should one overlook the Institute of Irish Studies, whose Director has for some years questioned the validity of 'the two nations' theory, and who, with very slender resources but with the help of generous colleagues, successfully launched a new degree course in Irish Studies.

All of these institutions are present here and do not need me to emphasise their importance to the enterprise we have undertaken. However, I may be allowed to make a special reference to the Linen Hall Library, Ulster's oldest cultural institution, and unquestionably part of the heritage of all of us whatever our religious or political affiliations. Those who founded the library in 1788 aspired to create here a community devoid of religious rancour, and one in which every cultural tradition would be encouraged and esteemed. They produced *Bolg an Tsolair,* a miscellany in the Irish language, organised the Belfast Harpers Festival and made possible the publication of Edward Bunting's *Ancient music of Ireland* in 1796. In the two centuries since then the Library has accumulated a collection of books, pamphlets, newspapers and documents that are a unique resource for the study of any aspect of Ulster or Irish life. The

Library is still committed to the ideals of its founders, and must have an importance for a cultural traditions group, if only as a civilised meeting-place for cross-community dialogue, common-ground at the very heart of troubled Belfast.

CHRISTOPHER NAPIER

On 19th June as he moved out of Belfast on his journey to the Boyne, King William III, of 'Pious, Glorious and Immortal Memory' was overtaken by a heavy shower of rain and sought the shelter of a big tree on the site of the present Cranmore Park. The tree in question was long honoured by the King's admirers until it was blown down in the violent storms of 1796. The memory of that tree lives on, however, in the name of the area 'Cranmore' which in Irish means 'the Big Tree'. How strange it may seem to some of us today that it is in the Irish language that these Admirers of His Majesty have perpetuated the memory of that event!

Likewise, when one looks for meaning in the chorus of one of the Orange Order's most famous songs, 'Lillibolero', one finds that it consists entirely of Irish, praising the Orange Lily and recounting how the day was won when the Lily was worn, an obvious reference to some skirmish or battle with some nationalists or Catholic group in the past.

Not of course that there is anything unBritish about the Irish Language. In Roman times the Irish Language was widely spoken in the North of England and throughout Scotland. Queen Boadicca, that personification of British resistence to the Roman Legions in the early years of the conquest might well have screamed as her battle cry 'Fag an Bealach' as she led her army to Colchester. That is not to say that she commanded the Dublin Fusiliers, the Connaght Rangers or the Royal Inniskilling Fusiliers, only that she, like they, raised a battle cry in Irish. But what is so strange in that? Under that later day namesake of Boadicca – her name means 'Victorious' – Queen Victoria, the Inniskillings and the Connaght Rangers helped to spread the British empire right around the globe. And, for many of them, Irish was their Mother Tongue.

During the first half of the nineteenth century Belfast was the Irish language capital of Ireland. Irish was taught in the Belfast Academy from 1794 and on the founding of the Royal Belfast Academical Institution under the Professorship of Dr William Neilson, Irish was taught there as a subject. The first printed textbook in the Irish language, *An introduction to the Irish language*, was published in 1808 by Neilson, and is suitably dedicated to His Excellency, Philip, Earl of Hardwicke, Lord Lieutenant General and Governor General of Ireland. This was the golden era of Belfast's literary life. The Linen Hall Library and the Natural History Society formed a centre around which medicine, science, literature, poetry and the investigation of history and legend flourished. A natural development of this was the establishment in 1828 of the very first Ulster Gaelic Society with the Marquis of Downshire as its President. Perhaps it was symbolic that the first literary task of that Society was to translate Maria Edgeworth's *Forgive and forget* into Irish. During the following years Belfast far outstripped Dublin in the publication of books, magazines and text books in the Irish tongue.

It was not unexpected then that when the corporation built St George's Market on behalf of the city, the city's coat of arms (still visible there today), should proudly proclaim 'Lamh Dearg Eireann' – the Red Hand of Ulster – that symbol of the Royal O'Neills of Tyrone which the City Fathers inherited from Conn O'Neill of Connswater fame – and the Lords of Clandeboye. Proud of its Irishness, proclaiming its legitimacy, its succession to the Gaelic Lords, Belfast struggled into the Industrial Revolution of the mid eighteen hundreds.

However, the Potato Famine, the bad politics of agrarian unrest and the growing strength of the Orange Order as a political force drove a wedge between English speakers on the one hand and the Irish speakers and their supporting cultural division on the other. The intervening century has done little to reverse this trend. The Irish speakers in Belfast and the surrounding districts have not gone away, the language continues to be taught, to be learned, to be talked and to be used as the language of the family and the cradle, utterly outside the realms of politics and religion notwithstanding repeated attempts by the warlords in each generation to hi-jack the language – or opposition to it – as part of their armoury against their political opponents. The victim of all of this, however, has simply been the language itself, and the culture that it supports.

However, what is the position today? Blowing aside the Celtic mists that are commonly seen to surround the whole of the language and culture issue, we see in Northern Ireland today approximately 60,000 people who either speak the language or have learned the language and have sufficient knowledge of the language to appreciate in part, if not in whole, the importance of the language as a key to unlocking the treasure chest of their culture and their history. Among the 450,000 odd who make up the political minority in Northern Ireland this represents in round figures at least ten per cent. Of that number only probably as little as one or two per cent are members of the majority community, but, if such a small percentage represent the majority community, it is only fair to say that many of those members have more than distinguished themselves in their fame and their achievements, dis-proportionate to their numerical strengths in the Irish speaking community. I can instance these if required.

When asked what my view is on the relationship of the minority community in general to the Irish language, I equate it to the sacred cows of India. There is no doubt that to 90 per cent or so of them the Irish language is a closed book, something they have only a very scant knowledge of or interest in but they generally wish it well. But if any outsider, either from England or from the majority community, were to attempt to denigrate, slight or interfere with the Irish language in any way, then there is a sudden rush-to-arms of otherwise disinterested persons to protect what they see as a valued part of their heritage, although they themselves are not prepared to put themselves out in the slightest way to investigate this heritage for themselves. The Department of Education can bear witness to this in the recent reaction to their White Paper on Education.

The constraint of the available time prevents me from going into detailed examples in any of the matters referred to. Perhaps it is sufficient to say by way of conclusion that I see the social unity of the people of Northern Ireland ultimately achieved by an appreciation of the traditions and cultures of each other. My feeling is that there is a very much wider acceptance of the loyalist/Unionist/Orange tradition among the nationalist population than the reverse. The founders of the Ulster Gaelic Society of 1828 saw the Irish language and culture as a ready means for bringing together the two traditions within the island of Ireland. I believe that their view still holds true today. There is in embryo within the Irish speaking community of Northern Ireland a harmonious interface of two traditions where each, proud of their own, is pleased to examine and respect the traditions of the other, without fear of domination or ambition of conquest. At the moment I see among the members of each community living in rural areas a much greater awareness of the tradition and culture of the other community than exists in the cities.

I would welcome any ideas which could come forward today which would help to break down the impenetrable wall of 'not wanting to know' that exists widely among certain sections of both communities in relation to each other.

DAVID TRIMBLE

The object of this conference, is to discuss how diverse traditions can exist. I think the chairman's introductory comments touched on some very important issues of a general nature to which we will have to address ourselves. There are certain diversities here and I will come back to what they might be in a moment. We have to decide, however, whether or not we are just a gathering of nice good civilised people meeting in this hotel far away from the city streets and the sort of ugly scenes pictured on the front page of the *Independent* this morning,* engaged in mutual appreciation and self-congratulation. Of course, that is not our proper activity but there is the danger that in gatherings of this nature, the reality outside will be forgotten. Jack Magee has said that the modern historiography has scarcely penetrated the schools. I would add that it is not yet to be seen anywhere on the streets.

There is, I think, another danger to be avoided. That is inappropriate attempts to integrate existing diversity. One should not try to blend together traditions that are essentially different. We may disagree as to the extent of those differences, but there is little to be gained by trying to meld things together. Our object is to discuss how diverse traditions can be affirmed and enjoyed. We must not forget about affirmation, for an attempt to prevent or inhibit that affirmation will simply create problems. We should not be afraid of difference. The chairman's introduction made the valuable point that diversity can be tolerable. There are many countries and societies which do have within them tremendous diversities in cultural terms, without those differences necessarily resulting in conflict. It is when some antagonistic policies evolve in relation to those cultures that conflict occurs. If I may say so, the picture that Christopher Napier gave us of Gaelic studies in early nineteenth century Belfast emphasises that point. At that time there were no antagonistic policies and the hostility displayed in some quarters

---

*Coincidently that paper had carried a not untypical photograph of a scene in Belfast in which a member of one 'tradition' graphically displayed his contempt for the other.

towards Gaelic today stems from the time when the Gaelic movement was largely taken over by people with a particular set of
policies. It will be a very hopeful thing if that ceases to be the case.

While we should be prepared to recognise diversity and affirm it,
we ought also to be fairly rigorous in our approach to it. If there are
problems they should be faced, for there will be no long term benefit
in pretending that they do not exist. In this context the title of this
group concerns me. What does the term 'traditions' actually mean?
We have had various euphemisms for the divisions that exist. We
have talked about 'divisions in the community', 'the two communities' and now we are talking about 'the two traditions'. This last
phrase, it seems to me, is more coy, more circumspect and perhaps
more meaningless than the earlier euphemisms. We do have to try to
identify the nature of the groups we are discussing. This will lead to
problems. I think that Jack Magee and I may disagree on this, for I
noticed with interest his criticism of the two nations theory, which I
consider to be a more honest approach than that which talks merely
of the two traditions.

We also need to be careful of what we mean by the term 'culture'.
It is worth asking whether there are, and to what extent there are,
different cultures within the British Isles. I use that term deliberately
to avoid yet another euphemism. Within the British Isles we all
speak English, though some people in Scotland and Wales and a
smaller number in Ireland also speak other languages. The media
we enjoy – newspapers, books, television – are largely the same.
There are some regional differences, in varying extent, in some
areas, but I would suggest to you that there is an underlying unity in
the culture of the British Isles as a whole. To take a small example:
part of the reason for the recent difficulties experienced by the *Belfast
News Letter* is the uncomfortable fact that the protestant working
class in Belfast much prefers the *Sun* which consequently outsells the
News Letter in Belfast. This preference is specifically for the *Sun*,
rather than its rival the *Daily Mirror*. In Belfast the latter has a
largely Catholic working class readership. Ulster is regarded as
being different from the British mainland yet in Ulster the predomi-
nant circulation is of national papers. In the Republic of Ireland the
difference is more marked, but one only has to look at the size and
direction of television aerials to see a clear and obvious element of
cultural unity. These points are made, not to deny the existence of
differences, but to point out that the differences that do exist are not
as marked as in some other divided societies.

One turns now to consider, briefly, the nature of the two compet-ing cultures that are generally regarded as existing here. The term I use to describe the culture I grew up in is 'Ulster-British'. I do not like using the term 'Protestant' because of the sectarianism encou-raged by the use of religious labels. One must, however, be honest and recognise that historically community identity and national consciousness were very often formed through religion, (and that not just in the British Isles), with the result that the use of religious labels is sometimes unavoidable. Of the alternatives to religious terms often used, the term 'Ulster-Scot' is not accurate, if only because it leaves out the not insignificant English settlements in Ulster and the term 'planter' is also inaccurate, for only a few of the Anglo-Scottish immigrants were actually planters and, more importantly, it also omits the 'native' Irish who were and have been absorbed within the cultural community that has developed here.

The term Ulster-British is also to be preferred because it empha-sises the point that we do not see ourselves as a self contained community unique to this little bit of narrow ground. We are part of a larger grouping, and I was particularly pleased to hear the references by Michael Longley to Scotland. Particularly in East Ulster, in any examination of culture, identity and perception, the very strong connections with northern England and Scotland stand out. Around the Irish Sea there is a triangle consisting of Liverpool, Glasgow and Belfast. This triangle is significant in terms of the economic development of those areas: their growth and decline have been linked and the local cultures are also strongly linked. One only has to mention the following in Ulster for Liverpool and Glasgow football teams to make the point. So the Ulster-British people are not a separate people but part of a larger grouping, modified or affected by their particular historical experience here.

There is, then, an asymmetry between the Ulster-British culture and what for want of a better word one will call the Irish Gaelic/ Catholic culture. The latter has, in the course of the last century or so, tried to develop, or redevelop, its own self-contained culture. It was clearly bound up with the development of political separatism. It was to be 'ourselves alone' politically, culturally and, or, especi-ally, linguistically. But it has not entirely succeeded for the reality of culture in the Republic of Ireland is a sort of compromise between Ireland's British heritage and the Gaelic/Catholic cultural aspir-ations of the separatists. The persistence of British influences in the Republic and the existence of Gaelic/Catholic influences within

Ulster can blur the picture. Yet there is a clear difference between the Ulster-British and Gaelic/Catholic cultures.

The compromise in southern culture mentioned above is an uneasy one for it scarcely exists in the rhetoric of the State which is virtually exclusively Gaelic/Catholic. The rhetoric also creates a problem in the relationship between the two cultures. This is an awkward problem to mention at a conference where one wishes to be positive but it cannot be avoided. The rhetoric and sometimes the practice of Gaelic/Catholic culture has not fully recognised the existence of the Ulster-British culture. It is not just that it seeks to assimilate another culture: it sometimes refuses to recognise even the existence or validity of that other culture, trying to downgrade the divergence to purely religious differences or to merely regional variations within one culture. Too often it is suggested that if unionists or orangemen were properly educated or indoctrinated he would perceive his 'Irishness' and even realise the Gaelic culture was 'his' culture as well. I even got a dose of this ridiculous proposition last night when I was demurring at the unbalanced musical entertainment that was presented to us. This attitude is quite objectionable and it does create difficulties for co-existence between cultures when one culture is sometimes not prepared to recognise the existence of the other or engage with it on its own terms. Any form of co-existence must acknowledge the right of each culture to exist and to perpetuate itself.

The failure to deal fairly with each culture even affects the modern historiography. I greatly enjoyed Roy Foster's talk last night and his book *Modern Ireland* is a considerable step forward. It is a very enjoyable read and it goes a long way toward recognising the distinctiveness of Ulster and that is appreciated. But too often it seems to me that the book does not accord equality of treatment to the Ulster-British and to unionism. Reference to Unionist leaders is invariably demeaning. Carson is portrayed as a lawyer on the make (page 465), Craig is unimaginative (page 465) although his achievement in the period referred to (1912–14) was anything but that. On the other hand, 'The Parnell era achieved epic status' (page 426) while the anti home rule campaign, which is epic for us, is described as hysterical, and the Unionist clubs, the ordinary constituency structure of the Unionist party, are called extreme (page 464). The Unionist view of home rule is also described as 'ludicrously extreme in retrospect' (page 470). Was it so extreme when 'the new regime was in a very real sense confessional' (page 534) and de Valera, by 'institutionalising a powerful Catholic ethos' . . . 'demonstrated to Ulster Protestants that the institutions of a united Ireland would be oppressively Catholic' (page 545)? In the light of these three quotations from *Modern Ireland* the reference to Unionist opposition to home rule as being 'ludicrously extreme' does seem a little strange.

There is still a long way to go before the historical experience of the Ulster-British community is treated in a similar way to that of others. This brings me to the one prospective part of this talk. Michael Longley talked of past neglect in his own experience. My upbringing was similar – until I was seventeen I received no formal education about Ulster or Irish history – all I knew I learned from my grandmother who, as a person brought up in Derry was very anxious to see that I had a proper awareness of the great siege and, of course, one learnt from reading Orange banners and the gossip of children. That past neglect was wrong and it has had a greater impact on one community than the other. This does need to be rectified, but I do not think that the modern or revisionist Irish historiography has yet tackled the matter properly. I would like to see a thorough study not so much of Irish history as of Ulster history. The reason for emphasis on Ulster is that any Irish history book, whether traditional or revisionist, is invariably written from the standpoint of a person located as it were in Dublin and surveying events as they appear from that location. Every now and again the north east comes over the horizon and then goes down below it. It comes up in the seventeenth century then disappears until, towards the end of the eighteenth, it pops up again. Then, a few years later, it goes down below the horizon until 1886 when it comes up again. This description may seem to be a caricature, but it does reflect the general approach. What is needed and what could with value be put alongside that general approach, is a history that takes the north east as its focus. The notional observer of events could be located in Belfast or Armagh and events could be recorded as they might have been experienced or perceived by the communities there. That would I think bring into focus the autonomous development that did take place there and it would correct the imbalances that arise from events being looked at and considered in terms of their significance in the development of the Dublin based community.

For example, one often picks up an Irish history book to see a disproportionate amount of space given to the Belfast United Irishmen while little space is given to the contemporaneous development of the Orange Order. Yet for Ulster the latter is historically much more important. Moreover the same book will probably ignore the Hearts of Steel agitation, which while not as important as orangeism, was more important in the social and economic development of Ulster than the United Irishmen. To take another example: the uniting of the Synod of Ulster and the Secessionist synod in the General Assembly of the Presbyterian Church, and the great revival, are much more important than the events which gave birth to the non-subscribing church. Yet the latter are trotted out regularly to the almost total exclusion of the former.

Jack Magee mentioned the preparation of teaching materials on a joint basis, presumably in order to get the two different viewpoints on events. That is a good idea, except that one of those viewpoints has not yet been properly stated and a lot of fairly basic research has still to be done. An Ulster based history would be a valuable study in its own right. But it would be a mistake for that history to proceed as if Ulster was a single or unique unit. That history must be put in its wider context. The Irish and British dimensions to our history have been mentioned. A European dimension also exists and indeed a study of European history would be valuable in other ways. I would hope that people who have some familiarity with the thirty years war in Germany would take a slightly more balanced and detached view of the war of the three kingdoms. When those events are compared it should be appreciated that there was nothing particularly unique or particularly nasty in seventeenth century Ireland. Indeed those events, bad as they were, did not match the barbarism displayed in contemporary Europe. It would be useful for all of us to be able to view matters in that context.

I would like to return to my worry about titles and refer to the keynote lecture on *Varieties of Irishness* which may be setting the wrong agenda. My final comment, to the Cultural Traditions Group, is that you must take care as to the way in which the work you are trying to do is perceived in the wider community. One of the enduring folk memories of the Ulster-British people is the fear of massacre – the fear that the people may cease to be, at least culturally. If the work of this Group is seen as having an agenda that refers to Irishness and the creation of a modern inclusive Irish nationalism, then this Group will find itself talking largely to itself and perhaps only to one tradition and not to the wider community that it must also address.

GENERAL DISCUSSION

Chairman

We have had four excellent speeches of a very frank and honest nature which certainly get the ball on to the pitch in an effective way. We have got about half an hour for general discussion at this stage. Could I suggest that we confine ourselves so far as we can to the broader themes because there will be plenty of opportunity in the seminars to look at the more detailed points. They may be themes suggested by Dr Foster yesterday evening, or by the speakers or, indeed, themes suggested by the private lucubrations of the members of the conference. Speakers might also want very briefly to signpost issues which the seminars might look at in detail, but we want to get as broadly representative a spectrum of views as possible.

Charles Fitzgerald: Belfast Newsletter

All this morning and all last night, there has been one thing very obvious in this gathering so far and it is that in this title 'traditions' we are looking backwards. The first time I heard anyone look forward in any sort of way, was David Trimble. I think if we are going to look backwards for the rest of this conference, we might just as well stay back. The history we have been speaking of is being made at this moment. The history which concerns us has yet to be made, and all of us here in Northern Ireland are going to be a part of it. And when you get out to Ahoghill and Cullybackey and elsewhere, they have as much to do with making that history, even though they cannot understand it, as in any other area of Northern Ireland.

Now about this Ulster/Scots/British culture thing. It is only as British as it suits a certain section of the Northern Ireland people to be British. The Protestant culture in Northern Ireland, to a large extent, is so short (in historical terms) that we must look and see how it compares and exists in time in contrast to other cultures. And there is a lot more to the present and to Ulster culture than just Protestant, Catholic, Nationalist and Unionist culture as they are proclaimed.

At the end of the day, much of today's protestant Ulster is desperately searching for an identity, because it isn't really sure if it ever
has had one of its own. It does not know (and has not known) from
one day to the other whether it is totally British, British-Irish,
Ulster-Irish, Anglo-Irish, Ulster Scot, Scottish-Irish or anything
else either.

A. T. Q. Stewart: Queen's University, Belfast

I must say that this morning I have felt encouraged, largely
because of the introduction which Dr Quigley has given us, distinguished by that brilliance with which I have been familiar for a long
time – since we were undergraduates in the same school of History at
Queen's. For the sake of brevity let me take up just one point from it.
I think there must be times when we all envy, and wish to understand, the means by which other nations, and other cultures, *seem* to
have overcome the particular kind of problem that we have, and Dr
Quigley has been much impressed by the American experience. At a
certain point in one of my courses, I ask my students to consider the
impact of the American War of Independence on Irish politics. It is
relatively easy to draw the obvious parallels between the American
and Irish situation in 1775; but it takes them a little more time to
think of the *differences*. It is the same in this context. I should like to
draw attention to two differences. America is, to say the least, larger
than Northern Ireland. The problem we have might there be
confined to a small peninsula in New England, and might not make
the national headlines, let alone arouse world attention. Secondly,
and more significantly, the United States has, as Dr Quigley says,
been from 1775 on the road to the New Jerusalem. It looks to the
future. (It has, of course, long since lost its way). But here in Ireland
we are trying always to get back to a Golden Age in the past. The
trains are travelling in opposite directions.

Maurice Hayes: Ombudsman

I think it would be worth while bearing in mind or getting some
sense of proportion of what we are about. I was extremely encouraged by the talks this morning and I think particularly by David
Trimble's at the end because it did pose questions and difficult
questions for us. But you know we are not actually changing the
world, we do not have any power to change the world, I do not think

we should begin to claim that sort of thing. I don't think we are going to wrap the whole thing up and come out with answers at the end of it all. I mean these great cultural debates are resounding: I find it very easy, actually, to get from B to Z, the real problem is getting from A to B, and I think David exemplified that. Even by the name that you take for yourself, you become labelled some way, and it is a great problem if you called yourself the ABC group, why wasn't it XYZ, the alpha/beta/gamma, ailm/beith or whatever it might be, but I think what as a member of the Group I was concerned with, was to begin a discussion of some of these issues in a way in which people would not feel threatened. Most of the cultural discussions that have taken place have been assertive, they have been to some degree triumphalist on both sides, and they produced an answering defensiveness on the other. What I would like to see, in some sense, is an opening up of this reservoir of separate, shared, differently perceived experiences, to see what is in it for all of us. I think we are just throwing a stone into the pool and wondering where the ripples will bring it to. I don't think it is any more significant or any more profound than that.

Terence Brown: Trinity College, Dublin

I would like to say that the studying of cultural traditions is often undertaken in the conviction that both traditions are benign and that if you understand your tradition you are necessarily going to produce benign effects. It seems to me important in the two cultures in Ireland, if there are two, and in the two cultures in Ulster, that it should be recognised at the start that there are malign aspects of both, and that to explore the nature of the malignity as well as the benign aspect is a part of the enterprise, otherwise the cultures that will be resurrected, will have a kind of partiality, and ineffectiveness. The nature of the exercise must be truly critical if it is to be essentially worthwhile.

Robin Wilson: *Fortnight* Magazine

I would like to carry on from something that Terence Brown just said which is very important. If we are talking about accommodating cultural traditions, we have got to be quite careful as to how we define that. At its best, it entails the praise of pluralism as an alternative cultural agenda and policy as Michael was talking about earlier on. At its worst, however, it can be a straightforward accommodation of sectarianism. It can accommodate precisely the notion that there are two monolithic traditions on this island, and it is crucially important that we distinguish the notion of accepting difference from the idea of praising diversity. Accepting two different traditions is one thing, and there are all sorts of problems with it. But praising the idea of diversity, that there are in fact several different traditions – and several different cultural influences in Ireland which have very little to do with Ireland at all – is a key part of making any progress.

The other point I would like to make, again linked to what Terence was saying, is that another danger in this kind of debate in the North is that an almost complete relativism can be applied: that either what everyone thinks is fine, on the one hand, or on the other hand that anything anybody thinks that is linked up to 'the two traditions' is just a sectarian shibboleth. Thus, for example, if people in West Belfast complain about house searches, they may not be complaining because they are dyed in the wool nationalists or republicans whose views ought to be moderated slightly, but because they are having their doors kicked in at eight o'clock in the morning. There are things like that where one cannot simply take these cultural traditions as a whole without unpacking them – without picking out the good, the bad, the reasonable, the unreasonable, and so on – because otherwise one does not have any real purchase on them at all in terms of bringing about any kind of change.

The final thing I would like to say is that in Dr Hayes' comment, which shows another danger in this concept, there is almost a pessimism to begin with. There is almost a sense of 'well, there are those two traditions out there and really they are going to go on regardless of what we say in this room and we might as well face that'. Again, that is an understandable feeling, but it is a dangerous one – we do need to think about alternative agendas. We do need to think about a situation where we are not always reacting against that definition of what the agenda should be, because if we do that we will always be meeting in this kind of situation in this kind of room and feeling rather powerless.

Brian Lambkin: Lagan College, Belfast

I have been struck by the secular tone of the remarks of speakers so far, I am slightly perturbed by it. If the problem that we have set ourselves is to find ways towards achieving unity in diversity, it seems to me the appeal that has been made so far is to the American method, which is appeal to a secular myth. I would hope that we would have regard in our deliberations to the religious dimension to this question as well, and to the fact that the cultural institutions which possess the most powerful myth in this regard are the Churches, – I refer to the notion of the Trinity, the idea of the prayer of Jesus at the Last Supper that they may be one, Father, as we are one. All I am asking is that in our deliberations the religious dimension be considered as well as the secular.

James Hawthorne: Former Controller, BBC Northern Ireland

I want to confess to a difficulty left unsolved, even after twenty-seven years in broadcasting! One of the difficulties in trying to show the broad spectrum of our community culture, or simply to represent the usual two sides of our community, is that there is what I would call a difference in 'texture' between those two stories. If one was, let's say, trying to popularise Irish History, for example, making educational programmes for schools about Irish history, there was a basic problem to solve.

Suppose for example you include music. A song which 'kicks the Pope over Dolly's Brae' has less of a dying fall than 'The Bold Fenian Men' or 'Kevin Barry'. In other words, one side of our story is more attractive to tell than the other. And let's be fair, one side is more attractive to journalists than the other. Journalists from outside the Province have come here and found a place in ferment. A journalist – and indeed an artist – is concerned with change and he finds what he is looking for more in one side of the community than in the other. One side has at least a greater aspiration for change and there is therefore a more attractive story to investigate and tell.

But what of the side of the community that holds to old values – values that are becoming less and less well regarded? Their story is less attractive, more difficult to tell and they do not get as good a showing. And there's no easy solution to that problem. If I might give you a quick anecdotal illustration of what I mean; when I was producing BBC radio programmes for schools on history – partly speculative history because the programmes were dramatised and we had to imagine what O'Neill might have said to O'Donnel in a distant century as they contemplated battle – we had actors playing the parts. Of course the actors knew no history themselves, so when we did what might be called a 'green' programme the actors were deeply absorbed and stunned to sadness over the coffee break. And they would say things like: 'Jimmy. Did all that really happen?'

Now when we did an 'orange' programme – say, the 1912 period, the fight against Home Rule – we would have approached the story using the same techniques and I hope with the same good intentions. We would feature the speeches of the time and the songs. And what happened? The cast fell over themselves laughing! There was something in that particular integrity which they found strange, unattractive, even ridiculous, certainly amusing.

So I think we should admit that there is a real problem in telling both sides of our story with equality. One side seems to have a natural advantage over the other. And it's a problem I fear we must address.

Edna Longley: Queen's University, Belfast

I was very interested in David Trimble's speech, because I think he was asking questions, and questioning names and definitions and I think that is very much part of our problem. Speaking from the point of view of a critic of literature for instance, and I know this is looking much further ahead than Maurice Hayes might want us to look, the very concept of what *is* Irish literature is very much under scrutiny. And I think there has been this fear among Unionists, Protestants, of the very term 'Irish', although contradictorily they are not worried about the term 'Northern Irish'. It is certainly true that Irish literature, like other cultural manifestations in Ireland, has often been appropriated by Nationalist ideology whether in the Republic or in the North. Whereas the actual literature itself does not at all bear out or subscribe to that appropriation, and even what James Hawthorne was saying just now, although he was talking about history rather than literature, is strangely out of date for somebody who comes like me from the Republic, but has lived in Northern Ireland. So I know how much concerning history and the understanding of literature is in fact in a slow process of being revised and interrogated there. And I think Unionists need not be frightened of what is coming from that quarter, because there is change on the cultural front if not yet fully on the political front, and they might find that revisionists in Dublin (not only historians) were much more in agreement with them, than they realise. It is because of this fear, there is wincing away from something that might be 'Irish', whereas the term Irish, is absolutely neutral I think. In our context, it applies to what emanates from this island, and I find for instance the alternative, 'are you Irish or British?' is a totally false alternative, because 'Irish' is both an identity and also an allegiance, 'British' is only an allegiance and one can be Northern Irish and British, Scottish and British, Welsh and British. Can I put in a plug for *The Irish Review?* Bernard Crick has a very interesting article in the current issue called 'An Englishman examines his passport' in which he interrogates all the prevailing cultural definitions in the British Isles. David Trimble referred to Scotland: look at the shaking up that is occurring there.

Peter Woodman: University College, Cork

As you might gather from my accent I come from about 250 miles North of the River Lee.

I would like to address my remarks to David Trimble's contribution. There is one particular point that I would like to make. He was talking about the British contribution and the need to move away from the concept of the Ulster Scots, as there is a diversity of traditions coming in from the other Island which we have often over-simplified and neglected. I think it was interesting that at the same time when he was looking towards the 'other' tradition, he was doing something that is fairly common, particularly here in the North, and that is to perceive of the tradition over the Border as being something really based in Dublin. I have found that, having actually lived in Cork for the last six years, one of the things that really surprised me was that there is an equal richness and diversity of cultural traditions within the South of Ireland. Today this can actually be seen at a local history level. I suddenly found myself having to learn about all sorts of people. Having been brought up with the MacDonnell's, the O'Neil's, I now have to learn about O'Sullivan Beare or Grainne Bhaole who are as much part of local traditions within regions in the South of Ireland as we had here in the North. This diversity also occurs even today. I think that De Valera's concept of the 'Comely Maidens' dancing at the cross-roads, that concept of actually developing a particular type of Gaelic Ireland, has failed, but that underneath that we still do have this regional diversity which many of us living outside Dublin feel does not get its fair play. So we have to realise that we can also see Ulster's cultural heritage as one of a whole series on this Island, not merely as one alternative out of two, but only as one out of many.

Shane Belford: Northern Ireland Tourist Board

The Chairman has called me 'Shane', but I grew up in Bally-money (near Cullybackey!) being called Sean. My father came from Ballycastle in the north and my mother from Cork in the south and I guess they must have compromised!

I am being slightly flippant but could I make a little plea, and I hope I am not being too naive when I say that I would prefer to call myself Ulster/Bri-Irish. And I hope that while we want to make sure that we keep the differences between us, please is it possible to be a little bit of everything as well? Can I not have a foot in both camps please, culturally?

President-elect John Kennedy, when he was re-writing his inaugural speech, took out the word compromise and put in photo-finish. I live in Ireland and I am Irish. I have more in common with a man from Cork than I have with a man from Kent. I can't help it and he can't help it. But I am very happy here. I don't have any problems with identity or split-personality. I just love being in Ireland and being of its culture. I am happy here.

Chairman

On that note of general happiness, which hopefully is shared by most of us, maybe even all of us, it is a good time to break off. But before I do, could I say that when we re-convene as a full group we will not have Roy Foster with us. Although I conveyed what I hope were very warm thanks to him yesterday evening, I would like just to say again on your behalf how much we have all enjoyed having him here. He got the conference off to a tremendous start. The buzz of talk about what he said, that has been around the conference since then, and the references that have been made this morning to his lecture are evidence enough that he has given us all a good deal to think about. Not necessarily everything has commanded agreement, but certainly he has stimulated discussion and debate. Roy, since you will not be here, and since, if you had been, I would have wanted to give you a word in the afternoon, you are very welcome to say anything you want to say, even if all you may want to do is to say farewell.

Roy Foster: University of London

Thank you very much for that unexpected chance and for your words. What I will not use my three minutes for is to reply to David Trimble's remarks, although he got me wrong on one or two issues.

The one thing I would take up is that I *deliberately* used the loaded word 'nationalism'. I am not such an innocent that I did not know what particular heckles it might raise, and the particular associations it has, but I was arguing strongly and would argue again for a redefinition of the word which does not imply the political overtones which it carries. And I was very pleased with what Edna Longley said, as I so often am, in terms of using the word Irishness with an ease which is commoner in the South than the North: but which I think is something we should aspire to again in a politically value-free (if there be such a concept), way. Like Tony Stewart, I was very cheered and in some ways excited by what has been said this morning; and having read Tony very carefully for a long time, when something happens to cheer *him* around here, we can all have cause for optimism. Thank you.

PART III

CONFERENCE SEMINARS

REPORTS AND DISCUSSIONS

INTRODUCTION

The conference delegates divided into seminar groups, each with a reporter, to discuss education, the arts, communications and local studies. Each seminar had a list of suggested topics to be addressed, but were free to introduce areas of discussion which were felt to be crucial or relevant. They were asked to direct their debates with the objective of making specific recommendations.

At the end of the conference all the delegates met in plenary session, and the chairman of each seminar presented a summary and the recommendations of his group. This was followed by a brief open forum, with delegates raising specific issues which were addressed by the Cultural Traditions Group Chairman, James Hawthorne. The conference chairman, George Quigley, concluded the conference.

EDUCATION GROUP I

Chairman: Sean Fulton

Professor of Education, Queen's University of Belfast

Report to conference

We tried to discuss first of all the aims of education in a relatively focussed kind of way. We asked ourselves what was the purpose of education in relation to what one might call a divided society. The schools, universities and other educational institutions have additional responsibilities in a society like Northern Ireland, additional to what they have elsewhere or different from what they have elsewhere in perhaps more integrated communities. We came to the conclusion, as Jack Magee said this morning, that education has a limited but nevertheless very important role. Educational institutions should not only transmit information but allow their students and pupils the opportunity to explore that information, to reflect on what has been said to them and to try to identify what its meaning is for them. It was suggested by members of our group that this particular process or exercise cannot be value or culture free. That was our starting point.

There were a number of interesting individual points that came out of the discussion which followed. I have not time to mention them all. The question of structures was looked at and it was held that of course these were important. We have three types of schools, we have what one might call the state sector, the maintained sector and the integrated sector and one point of view expressed in the group suggested that there should be equality of funding between them. Others felt that there it was generally recognised, not least by those outside the state sector, that the voluntary principle and the resulting independence should be reflected in the pattern of funding. However, every one agreed that it was important that there should be relationships of trust between those who work and study in each of these particular sectors.

The second matter we examined was contact between groups, the method of making contact and the status of that contact. We also considered that not only inter-community but intra-community contact was both necessary and desirable in order to ensure the development of understanding. One particular issue highlighted the questions of mutual understanding and inter-community contact, namely the Irish language. Although only a small percentage of the minority community, 10% was the figure suggested this morning, use it in their everyday lives, it is identified with the minority community and any criticism of attempts to expand the use of Irish will be considered by almost all of that community as an unacceptable attack. Equally, aggressive attempts at development will be considered by many in the majority culture as an attack on them, although there appears to be a small but, nevertheless, significant demand for the teaching of the Irish language in the controlled sector.

It was generally accepted by the group that openness to other cultural influences is most easily achieved by those who are secure in their own culture. One of the most important questions for education relates to the difficulty of balancing the expression of identity with one culture without inducing apprehension in the other. It was pointed out that teachers must learn to cope with this difficulty in relation to both their pupils and themselves. In carrying out this task teachers need help – 'cushioning' was the word used by one member of the group – and the quality of teacher education both at initial and in-service levels is crucial.

Then we turned from these rather grand issues to the four issues that we were asked to look at. The first was the promotion of contact between young people of different traditions. In respect of types of contact, modern psychological research appears to suggest that if one wants to influence group attitudes at the group level inter-group contacts are much more effective than simply inter-personal. As we were advised by the educationalists in our group, there are many schemes in existence at present to promote contact between groups. We think that the educational reforms will provide a welcome opportunity for new developments and one of those mentioned was in fact the European dimension. Developments in Europe over the last 30 or 40 years were referred to 'as a miracle of reconciling diversity and unity'.

Then we went on to discuss cultural diversity in the curriculum and in this area also interesting innovations are being introduced.

There is the new cross-curricular theme of cultural heritage, and we have no doubt that it will have a major role. We had a couple of members of the working group in our seminar, and they lifted the corners of the bale a little to let us know the aims and objectives. It was pointed out that not all teaching goes on in the classroom, and quite a lot of the work involved in cultural deversity will take place outside the schools.

We also discussed the role of adult education. We have no doubt that it has or should have an important place but that any expansion of the work done by adult education institutions is constrained by lack of financial support for education in cultural heritage. Those engaged in adult education pointed out that not all teaching goes on in the classroom and quite a lot of the kind of work involved in cultural diversity takes place outside. Both universities have developed continuing education programmes which are clearly relevant to the acquisition of knowledge of our cultural heritage. Those who have not had the opportunity to attend a university in their earlier years have been helped by the programme currently on offer. In this respect a little financial support from the Government would pay great dividends. We were also reminded rightly that research was extremely important for it provided the knowledge and the information necessary for us to develop effective strategies and courses. At the end we came back full circle to the fact that the teachers were the key individuals and their training and the experiences they undergo in training were absolutely crucial to the kinds of development that we would like to see in schools.

SEMINAR DISCUSSION: EDUCATION GROUP I

INTRODUCTION

The remit of the group was to seek to address the following topics.

TOPICS

1. The role of education.
2. Contact between young people from different traditions.
3. Cultural diversity in the school curriculum.
4. The Irish language in schools.
5. The contribution of tertiary education.

1. The role of education

In considering the role of education in a divided society there was both disagreement and some agreement. The discussion took place within the context of three basic points which permeated the groups' deliberations:

- On the one hand, education is not the sole preserve of the formal educational institutions.
- On the other hand, schools are only one agency of reform in society. That cultural diversity can exist (and that tensions can surface in overt conflict) despite the lack of such values being inculcated in the education system has been illustrated dramatically in recent weeks in the Soviet Union.
- Within the educational context the teacher was believed to hold the key position in respect of community relations and cultural diversity.

a. Information transmission and changing of values

Points made and issues discussed centered largely on the role of Northern Ireland schools in relation to the transmission of information and the changing of values. The advantages and opportunities presented by the imminent opening up of Europe were also aired.

Whilst the view that information by itself is ineffective in achieving attitude change was supported, the point was made that the primary role of schools is not merely to transmit information passively but also to discuss and question it. Furthermore, information transmission itself is not value free: school structures (selective, single-sex etc) are important and can skew the selection and transmission of information. Also, since the function of schools was posited to be to 'reproduce society', our concern is with the transmission of values and therefore to reduce prejudice and to reform values.

The group was in agreement with the proposal that information exploration in relation to cultural diversity must occur in the context of relationships if the participants are to move, as people, in new directions. Teachers, it was stated, should be models and not rivals for their pupils. Responsibility was said to lie on teacher-trainers to encourage teachers to take 'the widest view'.

b. Support systems

In order to enable teachers – and other professionals working with children and young people – to cope successfully with the difficulties inherent in attempting to adopt and encourage a pluralistic perspective, a plea was made for the creation of support systems for these adults who had themselves to learn to own cultural diversity. Since this process involved a great deal of fear, anxiety, hurt and frustration such workers, it was stressed, need cushioning and to be less pressurised for results. It was also the case that some compromise of our ideals is necessary in the classroom.

c. Teachers' influences and interests

The extent to which teachers actually influence the non-academic development of their pupils was questioned, as was the conscious awareness of teachers of the cultural and other values which permeate their school and those that they promulgate. Teachers' responsiveness to and industry in respect of recent curricular initiatives including Education for Mutual Understanding (EMU) was warmly praised and the point was made that much of the extra cultural traditions work was undertaken in teachers' own time. However, it was also stated that the system needs changing: while there is great sympathy among teachers in different schools for Education for Mutual Understanding type of activities, what is of vital importance to them is the enhancement of their promotion chances.

d. A new agenda

The suggestion that a major task was to re-evaluate the nature of values in Northern Ireland since they 'had gone askew' was well received. The proposal for 'a new agenda' for education was welcomed by some members of the group. This would be related to values concerned with survival and the need for a stable environment: economic awareness linked to the primary role of education in preparing young people for employment was said to be necessary in order to break down existing barriers. In support of this view the present eductional system was described as elitist and the observation was made that it 'misses' a large proportion of young people. In regard to the West Belfast Initiative, for example, it was stated that the role of education should be concerned primarily with preparing the young people of the area for the forthcoming employment opportunities in that part of the city – this, it was argued, should over-ride cultural traditions concerned. The relationship between education and the economy was seen to be important.

Whilst there was some agreement that education is effective only if it is congruent with, and an extension of, existing cultural values in a community, the approach of 1992 was said to be welcome. The opening up of Europe was viewed as providing the potential to change the parameters of the whole community relations debate in Northern Ireland; it was felt that it will bring a whole new dimension to the concept of cultural diversity and the meaning of relationships in Northern Ireland. The group was reminded of the benign influence of the European movement, which was depicted as a 'miracle of reconciliation' and an affirmation of cultural diversity within a larger whole.

2. Contact

In addressing the issue of promoting contact between young people from different traditions, the question of integrated schools featured large but the discussion also embraced issues concerning intra-community diversity (as well as inter-community differences); security in one's own culture and different types of contact situations.

There was some disagreement in the group between defence of the present education system and pleas to find ways of improving the structures and minimising the inequalities. There was tension between requests to increase the number and status of integrated schools and the view that a pluralist education does currently exist and will be enhanced in the near future in the legislation that will result from the current education reforms. The education reforms were seen as throwing up major questions and as offering a new dimension to the problem.

a. Integration confidence

In addition to encouraging cross-community trips to Europe and elsewhere, the point was made that young people need a secure environment at home: they should be liberated from their 'ethnic ghettoes' or 'enclaves' through contact in the educational setting. Teachers in inter-schools seminars have shown that they consider that interaction in the classroom between the different groups of pupils is vital. It was argued that if half of the equation is missing in the school, disjunctions will be highlighted. There will soon be Fair Employment legislation but the concepts embodied in this Bill, it was stated, are ignored in the schools. Within the European context, the friendliness of different groups in countries like France and Germany was attributed to the non-segregated nature of their education system.

After some disagreement, the view that all types of school should have equal treatment achieved support, with the rider that it was not unfair that the voluntary and independent sectors should involve some cost to the participants. There was disagreement over the extent to which the present system disadvantages certain types of schools, Catholic schools to some extent and integrated schools to a very large extent. The great financial strains and other burdens experienced by integrated schools was stressed. A need to equalise the present rivalries and tensions between the different school systems was also articulated. It was stated that a central system of integrated education was not practicable at present. Also, a question was posed relating to the limits to be placed on the freedom for young people to make friends with whom they like – the emphasis was on benign contacts.

b. Inter-group and intra-group differences

The view was stated that whilst there was a plethora of inter-tradition contact activities these were the tip of the iceberg only. Furthermore, intra-community differences in views and values were not adequately addressed by the institutions of that community. Some of these differences, particularly within the Protestant community, were described as producing harder, sharper questions.

Individual communities, it was said, must accept an integrated plurality within the school system.

In order to increase confidence in one's own culture it was stated that there is a need to re-examine cultural ethos at an institutional level but without diluting the traditions. The group learned that the Council for Catholic Maintained Education, which has only been in existence for a year, has deliberately not been using the word 'ethos'. The Council has established a special committee to promote Education for Mutual Understanding, which appreciates that real cultural and social involvement is necessary and that there need be no threat to identity. There was agreement that security in one's own culture is important. Also, a feeling of trust was said to lead to the situation whereby unity and diversity complement each other, whereas fear renders unity and diversity into opponents.

c. Interpersonal and intergroup contact

Different types of contact were briefly outlined. The importance of people from the two traditions meeting as members of the two groups rather than just as individual persons was stated. Allport's 1950s thesis about different types of contact situations remained a classic. However, contemporary social psychological theory and research illustrates that changes in intergroup attitudes ('them and us' as opposed to 'you and me') are more likely to be achieved through 'intergroup' contact – ie between Protestants and Catholics meeting as Protestants and Catholics – than through situations involving 'inter-personal' contact between individuals as individuals.

3. Cultural Diversity

In discussing the inclusion of cultural diversity in the school curriculum it was recognised that it is likely that developments in the schools in this regard are probably not widely known outside the schools. The extent to which the teaching of Irish history had changed in recent years was considered and it was accepted that much of this type of teaching takes place outside the classroom and the school. Once again, the teacher was seen to play a pivotal role.

A number of participants described their own school experiences regarding the learning of history. There was agreement that modern revisionist historiography had impacted more in schools than Jack Magee had intimated in his address. Mr Magee was also credited with a much greater positive influence regarding the teaching of history than he appeared to realise.

It was felt that the Cultural Heritage Group, with its concern for a shared culture coupled with distinctiveness, would play a major role. It was suggested that one simple approach would be to aim to have cultural diversity in all schools, by attempting always to consider alternative interpretations and perspectives – as evidenced, for example, in reports in different newspapers. Examples of approaches to the inclusion of cultural diversity in the curriculum were the involvement of people outside the school by integrated schools, and the Schools History Competition which involved a lot of extra-school teaching.

4. Irish Language
a. Value
In examining, within the educational context, the place of the Irish language in the cultural diversity of Northern Ireland and how it could be made more acceptable to the wider community, the discussion revolved to a large extent around the values inherent in the learning of the Irish language and the relative importance in the debate of the cultural and linguistic dimensions of the activity.

b. Speakers
It was noted that much of the talk on this issue concerned the language and not the people who speak it. The advantage of focussing more on the roots of the language and its early speakers was acknowledged since it is probably not widely known that the language in the past was used by both Protestants and Catholics; it was very strong among early Presbyterians. Also, it was stressed that there is value in recognising that the language currently should only be partially identified with the Republic of Ireland; there is merit in looking at present use of the Gaelic language outside Northern Ireland, for example at the Scottish islands only fourteen miles offshore, which are part of the triangle referred to in David Trimble's 'Ulster British' address. It was suggested that the promotion of Irish has suffered from the attitudes of some identification of the language with Sinn Fein. The group was told that most Irish speakers oppose Sinn Fein and also speak one or more languages.

The group learned about how Irish had been taught during the last few years on a voluntary capacity (at lunch-time) to sixth formers in a controlled grammar school in East Belfast with no opposition or hostility from either pupils or staff (including those with well-known loyalist connections). There was also a demand for the classes from younger pupils. The interested pupils spanned both linguists and a community relations group. The point was made that this activity was successful due to its voluntary nature and would be resisted if it were mandatory.

The view that in learning Irish one can retain one's religious affiliation and be enriched culturally has clear educational implications, but it was felt that interest should not be confined to education only; the status of the language in the wider community was considered to be important. The useful pioneering role played by the BBC's Irish programmes in helping to break down prejudices due to ignorance of the language was agreed. The question was posed, 'Is it chiefly important to interact with other people in Irish or with the culture?' It was agreed that the learning had to be purposeful.

c. Promoting the language

Views regarding the relative importance of the symbolic or cultural value of the Irish language differed but a number of participants in the group agreed that the value of learning Irish was both cultural and linguistic. It was admitted that while the language could be disruptive in the community – Protestants were content with 'tradition' but unhappy with 'cultural tradition' – it was an important element in the identity of a minority, as evidenced in the responses to the Government's recent White Paper on education. One approach would be to focus on the binding elements of Irish and then try to get them into the curriculum without causing offence. It was felt that the churches could do a lot more regarding the Irish language.

The linguistic skills and linguistic merits in learning Irish were described as the same as those involved in learning any European language, except that a foreign language is less tangible and more distant to the learner. The view that the value of beginning to learn such languages is greatly improved if it occurs in primary school, when children have a greater language learning facility, was supported. It was also claimed that if Irish is learned at an early age that it facilitates the learning of other languages but the shortage of suitable teachers was a serious problem. The utilitarian value of knowing the language was recognised but felt to be more limited, for example in terms of enhancing job opportunities, than other major contemporary European languages.

5. Tertiary education

a. The question of access

The principal point which emerged in the few minutes which remained to consider the role of tertiary education in promoting cultural diversity – and which received support from the group – related to the crucial importance of the universities having the capacity to provide a second opportunity to obtain access to 'relevant' courses, for example in Irish Studies or selected aspects of Social Science (in both of the universities). This was felt to be particularly important in short, general interest courses and in certificate and diploma courses ie at 'sub-degree' level.

The point was made that financial help should be made available to assist potential students, particularly those unemployed, to meet the high cost of the fees for such courses. It was suggested that a credit system could be established to take account of such courses. The present pre-occupation with assessment and qualifications was considered to mitigate against the opening up of valuable educational opportunities for general interest courses and for less well qualified students. It was noted that the Queen's University of Belfast was experiencing difficulties with the Masters course in Social Science in relation to Irish Studies and that a highly relevant course in the former Polytechnic was cancelled in 1973 due to a need to increase the entrance qualifications.

b. Research

It was agreed that it is of crucial importance to sustain and promote the research needs in the area in the universities.

c. Teacher education

The group had intended to consider teacher-education, particularly in view of its recognition of the central role played by the teacher in the whole community relations and cultural diversity arena, but time did not permit.

RECOMMENDATIONS: EDUCATION GROUP I

1. The role of education

i. Recognition should be given to the central role of teachers in relation to education for mutual understanding;

ii. Consideration should be given to equalising the treatment of different school systems;

iii. The involvement of teachers in activities promoting education for mutual understanding should contribute to their promotability;

iv. A greater emphasis should be placed in the curriculum on basic needs, including economic, particularly in areas of very high unemployment;

v. Support systems need to be provided for teachers and other professionals engaged in work directly related to education for mutual understanding and cultural diversity;

vi. Information exploration and discussion in relation to cultural divisions should take place whenever possible within the context of relationships;

2. Contact

vii. Steps should be taken to increase awareness, understanding and use of different types of contact – intergroup as well as inter-personal.

3. Cultural diversity

viii. Teacher trainers should encourage their trainees to take 'the widest view' whenever possible;

ix. Full advantage should be taken of the opportunities provided by the opening up of Europe in 1992 in order to further promote improved understanding and acceptance of cultural diversity;

x. Full advantage should be taken of the current Government reforms in education in order to further promote improved education for mutual understanding;

xi. Steps should be taken to increase awareness outside schools of the extent of work dedicated to cultural diversity.

4. Irish language

xii. Steps should be taken to increase knowledge and use of the Irish language by, for example, the media, the churches, the schools;

xiii. The teaching of European languages, including Irish, should begin in Primary school and more teachers of Irish must be trained to meet the need;

xiv. Consideration should be given to offering Irish on a voluntary basis to Protestant pupils.

5. Tertiary education

xv. Further and higher education should be encouraged to offer a range of courses, including non-assessed courses and a credit system, in a flexible way to permit greater access to courses at different levels that are directly relevant to cultural diversity, particularly for less well qualified students;

xvi. Financial assistance should be made available to enable unemployed people to benefit from such courses;

xvii. Research needs in relation to community relations and cultural diversity should be sustained and further promoted.

EDUCATION GROUP II

Chairman: David Harkness

Professor of Modern History, Queen's University of Belfast

Report to conference

We addressed four questions relating to contact, cultural diversity, the Irish Language and tertiary education. Regarding the promotion of contact between young people, I think most of us were in favour of integrated schools and thought they should be facilitated as much as possible, though we recognised that this was no panacea for the whole province. We thought that if teachers were to exchange and to teach in the classes of other schools and if classes were to exchange and meet there would be financial implications and the Department ought to be aware of this and make the money available. I am sure it is doing quite a lot already in this field. We talked about such competitions as exist to bring students together and we preferred those that involve working together towards some goal rather than competing against each other, projects that either mix up children or combine them in some way, and we would like to see those encouraged. Joint trips, such as going to the Armada exhibition together or whatever opportunities arise, are better than doing nothing at all. We were given interesting information on a Strabane project which may be illustrative of a number of projects among teachers that have been working away quietly and achieving a lot in terms of teacher contact, and in terms of producing curriculum material for schools in particular areas. Indeed the point was made that it is often best to think of the number of schools in a particular community, and how they can be brought together, to work together. The pay-off, not only within the schools but within the wider community, including people who have left school, should be considerable. Because so little of this has been done, it is too early to say what the benefit might be.

We had a distinguished representative of the European Studies Project with us and he talked about the capacity to communicate between schools even through electronic mail. Schools don't actually have to meet, initially. They can begin to communicate from a distance but of course residential exchanges which might follow from that, and indeed in this case residence in Europe itself, perhaps at the later age group, can be very useful. Another expert stressed that the best age for children to encounter each other is before puberty and more should be done at a younger age to bring children together. Someone asked the question 'Do we know what percentage of schools in our province actually have cross-community activities under way?' We felt that we ought to know that, and that targets ought to be established so that we could monitor the degree to which schools are having such contact, and indeed should work to raise the percentage having such contacts.

Turning to cultural diversity in the school curriculum, we did feel that this should be seen as a culturally based priority, it should not be a social engineering, or a political, or any other kind of exercise. It should be done through existing courses to ensure that children do encounter the perspectives of the other community, in literature, in language, in local studies or in whatever area seemed appropriate. If there was to be a programme, it should not be called Irish studies but something else, for example, Heritage Studies, and it should be the same programme for all schools, a point that was strongly made. There were reservations about the priority which trying to improve community relations should be given. It certainly was felt by some that in our peculiar circumstances it was a legitimate priority and we must not shy away from it. Cynics thought that some method of monitoring this whole field would have to be built to ensure that schools were actually delivering. Others pointed out that the new preoccupation with assessment of performance and the new emphasis of the inspectorate as inspectors, rather in the factory inspector sense, will ensure that schools are forced to participate fully.

Turning to the Irish language in schools, I think it was felt by all of us that this was an option which ought to be accessible for those who want it, rather than a compulsion upon those who did not want it. There is no problem about that view, but a problem was identified and that is that within the school system Irish does not share the same status as other contemporary European languages and there was plea that, particularly for those students who can only cope with one or barely cope with one other language, there ought to be the freedom to choose Irish and not to have to choose German or French or Italian. There was a strong feeling that our community needs to allow this, despite the fact that other arguments can be advanced, for example that to be marketable to find a job, students should have to do a modern European language first.

So, moving on to tertiary education, and the contribution that it can make, it was pointed out that a great deal was being done between the two teacher training colleges in Belfast and probably as much as could be, though there was a strong view expressed that although an attempted integration had failed in the past this should be tried again: that it was very important that teachers should be trained together even if the schools can not be integrated into a single system. Responsibility in adult education was also stressed and the point was made that in adult education in the Irish language, for example, there is no public support: that there is a range of twentieth century hedge-school equivalents doing their best in a variety of premises and places without proper financial support. Also there has not been proper financial support for initiatives in the Protestant community when it has chosen to try to explore its own heritage. Places like the Ulster People's College should have more support and indeed the universities were also asked to think of doing more to help in the field of adult education, to make material available and to think more about the needs of people teaching in adult education. It was felt that, within, the universities could probably do more to confront the fairly obvious segregation that goes on. Students may be taught in the same lecture theatres, they may be taught in the same tutorials but the rest of their time tends to be heavily segregated and perhaps the universities ought to do more to break that down and to stop dodging the issues that are uncomfortable or divisive and to confront problems which ought to be brought out into the open. And lastly, and this echoes one of the points that Sean Fulton made, one's actions could often be more important in one's own community. If one has an enlightened and progressive and tolerant viewpoint then it might be more effective if it was exercised in one's own community first, to try to bring that community along rather than simply aiming one's remarks at the other community.

SEMINAR DISCUSSION: EDUCATION GROUP II

INTRODUCTION

The Chairman began the seminar by suggesting that the group start with a general discussion of the purpose of education before moving on to specifics. The second education seminar led by Professor Fulton would be covering the same topics with the emphasis on practicalities. This seminar might take a wide ranging approach including the purpose of education and its strengths and weaknesses in the Northern Ireland context.

The seminar considered view that education in the present context was 'education to respect culture' and that meant removing fear. Theoretical approaches could not achieve this but personal self confession expressed our fears. Openness and personal assessments were of more value than theoretical discussion. Some conference members had felt threatened by what had been expressed at the conference so far. If even some of the group felt threatened, this indicated the sensitivities raised when discussing the interpretation of historical events.

TOPICS

1. Cultural diversity in the curriculum
2. The Irish language
3. Promoting contact between young people from different traditions
4. Tertiary education.

1. Cultural diversity in the curriculum

a. Content and process issues in the curriculum
The educational discussion was dichotomised into issues to do with the curriculum (issues of content) and issues to do with mutual understanding between the communities (issues of process). Follow-

ing general contributions from seminar members, the chairman summarised ways in which schools could access material for use in teaching heritage/history. These included a mixture of the content/ process approaches such as BBC archive material; generation of texts and materials etc by committed teachers already involved in collaborative ventures; increased use of folk museum materials; visits to exhibitions such as the Armada exhibition. Maximising the potential of existing sources and agencies was part of the task.

b. History teaching

It was felt that one of the most important subjects reflecting cultural diversity was history. A number of people described their personal, and unsatisfactory, experiences of being taught Irish history. They ranged from being taught what was thought to be a distorted view of Irish history, to being taught no Irish history at all. The group discussed how Irish history could be injected into the curriculum.

A pilot study of 18 schools, (six in each of the three jurisdictions of Northern Ireland, Great Britain and the Republic of Ireland), in the European Studies Programme was described. This was part of the work of a group looking at the preparation of an 'enlightened curriculum' in history and geography. This had resulted in the inclusion of a North American and a European dimension into history teaching. The aim was to introduce differing cultural dimensions and an awareness of the relativity of cultural values. It was explained that the schools in the programme were in contact with one another through computer links.

The group acknowledged that it must confront the reality that two views existed in Northern Ireland and that no amount of history teaching would change that. Doubts were expressed about the ability of history teaching to stimulate thought in pupils, rather than a mere accumulation of knowledge. For example – it was difficult to get adolescents to say what they thought in a classroom situation. History became the presentation of facts by pupils in a form that they felt was acceptable to the teacher. Teachers should not try to sanitise Ulster history.

The question was asked if anyone had experience of how pupils were reacting to new Irish history teaching. Did they react against it? Was there any evidence that it stimulated thought? No one knew of an objective data source but some anecdotal evidence was recounted. Occasionally parents had complained about certain text books.

Children tended to learn history for the instrumental purpose of passing an exam; this was stating the obvious but it raised the question of presenting history in an innovative way to young pupils. It was recognised fully that children may not incorporate what they learn in history classes into their value system. It was noted that the Department of Education is currently looking at the identity structure of pupils from different school types.

The group asked whether any progress was being made in involving parents in history teaching? It was thought this was a potentially explosive area. The extent of such involvement had not been determined. Legal requirements to teach certain topics could lead to state-funded school pupils being withdrawn and sent to an independent school. The independent sector, if expanding quickly, could adversely affect integrated schools.

In general discussion it was felt that pupils could shed the values of the school very quickly and to get them to internalise ideas and evaluate them critically required a well planned general strategy between schools, teachers and parents and a range of organisations.

c. **Religion in the curriculum**

Two group members noted that the group had discussed the curriculum a great deal without mentioning religion. What did the group think should be covered in this area and do current teacher stocks have the knowledge that would be necessary to teach such a subject?

The group agreed that lack of knowledge led to fear and that many people lacked any knowledge about the structure of the various churches. People were often unsure of the nature of current and historical associations between Church and State. This led to suspicion and mistrust. The group accepted that religion was one of the darkest regions in education. The curriculum certainly needed to be developed in that area. It was noted that in integrated schools, religion was taught as an academic subject.

2. The Irish language

It was agreed that a balanced view of culture was desirable. Some people felt that the Irish language had been associated with republicanism in the eyes of Protestants and that this was a perversion of the language and the culture.

a Accessibility

The availability of history/heritage teachers would be a problem if a policy of accessibility were to be implemented. One person knew of Protestants who had complained because Irish was not available in their school yet the Celtic department at Queen's University required 'A' level Irish an an entry qualification to some courses. A number of people had the perception that a 'sizable desire' existed among Protestants to learn Irish that was not always being met. The Celtic civilisation course at Queen's University was very popular and some of the students had gone on to take the linguistic option which was available.

It was pointed out that it was dangerous to concentrate too much on fluency in the Irish language. There was not enough emphasis on accessibility to other aspects of cultural heritage such as literature, poetry, place names and music. One group member gave an example of Irish scholars enshrining the Irish language by laying claim to certain esoteric aspects of Irish heritage. The example was that of ancient Irish law which, it was said, had been glorified and venerated out of all recognition. Key areas such as this needed to be simplified and brought into the open through publication of simple text books. By simplification and increasing the availability of translated texts, heritage could be taught accurately. Good simple translations were rare. Fergus Kelly's book, *A guide to early Irish law*, simplified a complicated topic. Some Celtic scholars accepted that there were texts that were inaccessible to most people but that was because the manpower needed to translate them was not available.

It was accepted that broadcasting had a role to play in making Irish literature and culture more accessible to the public in general and schools in particular. A number of radio programmes already disseminated information to a wide audience and had received a favourable public response.

b. Options

It was accepted that perhaps an 'option model' could be adopted in schools, offering a general course with the option of a linguistic element if desired (as in the university). Some people did not think it desirable to promote Irish in Protestant schools for a number of important reasons: firstly, there had been three arson attacks on the Celtic department at Queen's University; secondly, from the public relations angle schools wanted to attract pupils and not to deter parents on account of a policy of promoting the Irish language. Some people thought that a compulsory modern language may be a reasonable policy for the more able pupils who can handle more than one, but that in secondary schools Irish could be marginalised if students took only one language.

On this issue two points were identified. One was that the introduction of Irish on the same level as other languages could be divisive from a Protestant point of view, the other is that not introducing it in the same way as other languages could lead to Catholic perceptions of discrimination against what is to them a very important symbol.

Introducing another dimension to the discussion one group member pointed out that language learning had labour market implications. Already Catholics were disadvantaged by virtue of their tendency to take proportionately more arts "A" level subjects than science subjects.

In general the group felt that the option should be given – even if that led to compromising the person's chances of a job.

c. **Funding of Irish medium schools**

The group was informed that the Shaw's Road Irish School gets 100% of revenue costs and 85% of capital costs. At the moment no new Irish language nursery schools are being funded. This was not a matter of the particular language used in the school – there were simply no funds. It was noted that the teachers of the Irish school generate a lot of their own materials which reduces costs.

3. Promoting contact between young people from different traditions

The group felt that schools working together on local history projects was important and may have more effect than teaching Irish history to groups of pupils who were isolated from each other. A number of people said that in their experience a lot of teachers were very concerned about such links. A project already existed in Strabane which resulted in the production of a history text. This was a collaborative venture between Protestant and Catholic teachers. Its value had not been assessed. The fact that the materials had been developed by teachers of Protestants and Catholics was an innovation that produced a balanced outcome.

Some people thought that inter-school contact could be confrontational and generate conflict – an 'us against them' mentality. Mixing groups of pupils from different schools during inter-school contact was suggested so that they would not divide on religious lines. However the group was of the opinion that confrontation was inevitable, it was an integral part of the learning process. Competition would be welcome in this learning process.

The group seemed to be in favour of the idea of 'travelling teachers'. Teachers should promote inter-school teaching and resource sharing. There will be a lasting benefit if joint efforts are made. There could be some transport problems in bringing school children together for competitions/exhibitions. Teachers could go on residential 'curriculum exchange' courses.

Although it was known that in some areas prior to 1984 there had been no inter-school contact in some places, now progress was being made. An invitation to nominate EMU (Education for Mutual Understanding) representatives had been received positively by schools.

4. Tertiary level education

The group discussed the fact that Protestant and Catholic teachers are trained in different teacher training colleges. It was noted that one attempt to amalgamate Protestant and Catholic teacher training on a single campus had already failed. However, the colleges were already in contact through the EMU programme.

There was general agreement that there was a demand for adult courses in both the Irish language and heritage studies to be constructed and that steps should be taken to meet this demand.

RECOMMENDATIONS: EDUCATION GROUP II

The chairman summarised the group's discussions:

1. Cultural diversity in the curriculum

i. Materials for curriculum development are needed. The Strabane project shows that this is possible and that teacher enthusiasm generates materials cost effectively.

ii. A heritage studies element in the curriculum should be developed.

2. The Irish language

iii. The Irish language should be available as an unfettered option. Pupils should have the freedom to choose Irish even if only one language is to be taken. Such unfettered rights have implications for pupils entering the labour market.

iv. Adult education in the Irish language should receive financial support as should institutions promoting cultural education.

3. Contact between schools

v. Integrated schooling is viewed by the group in a favourable light and as something to be facilitated.

vi. An exchange of Protestant and Catholic teachers between schools has merit. This has resource implications.

vii. Competition between schools should be encouraged as should joint trips to museums and exhibitions.

viii. It would be desirable to get better information on the nature of and effects (on teachers and pupils) of contact between schools. Perhaps targets should be set for levels of inter-school contact.

4. Tertiary education

ix. There should be greater communication between the two teacher training colleges. Integrating the teacher training colleges should be tried again.

x. Universities should take more care to break down student self-segregation on their campuses.

xi. Universities have a role to play in making simple and appropriate texts available for adult education.

THE ARTS

Chairman: Maurice Hayes

Ombudsman

Report to conference

I have a sort of confession to make which is that we lost the questions. A more respectable formulation of that excuse would probably be that in any case they had been transmuted by the intensity of the artistic experience of the group and we arrived at something else entirely. Actually, what will be interesting is the number of echoes from the educational discussions and the number of times the themes that are common to the community development come through, of participation and empowerment and of starting where people are.

But starting where we were, we had difficulty with definitions and terms and a feeling that things like art, culture were a turn-off really for people and then we wondered, too, whether we should not talk more about arts or intellectual life in general, and whether it was not too constricting to limit the thing just to 'arts' as in the Arts Council programme and that things like sociology and other works had a part in enabling people to understand the life about them and their culture. There was also a confusion, we thought, even in our own minds, as to whether we were talking about art or culture. We thought, too, for a moment about the transcendant role of the artist in society as an interpreter and a codifier of experience and we thought this was tremendously important. Even more important was the need to enable the participation of people, in a sense helping people to have fun, to see what we are talking about as an enjoyable and enriching experience, instead of some sort of cultural calisthenics, you know, that is good for us. We discussed also the need to improve access to the arts and the ability to engage in the arts activity and resources, and this impelled us, I think, or a considerable number of us, to want to make a political statement about the general impoverishment of the arts in our society at the present time. Also, the importance of not being seen to be putting a drop in the bucket when someone else was pulling the plug out at the other end. Also, the general sort of impoverishment of artistic and cultural life by the pressures, the manifold multi-national pressures that come on people.

We also had difficulty in discussing the subject because in order to make it discussible, in order to produce the sort of report that we could knock off on our fingers here, it was necessary to put the thing into boxes and the feeling is that once you bureaucratise that sort of process it does tend to stultify development and discussion. We kept coming to the importance of education, of schoools, the importance particularly of further education. The importance of beginning where people are, in the community, pubs, clubs and what have you, of empowerment, of enabling people to participate. It should not be a question of dosing people but enabling them to be part of the whole thing. We were also struck by the absence, and it was mentioned this morning in a different way, of discussion about religion. We thought of the importance of religion as a component of cultural experience and many other things. We wanted to stress also that culture was a dynamic thing.

Then we get on from there to consider, within that framework, what sorts of things might be done, what are the good things? There are lots of good things going on, where they are being inhibited. Is it a resource problem? Is it a structural problem? Is it an attitudinal problem? One of the foci of activities we looked at was the Arts Centre. Why there should not be an Arts Centre on the same basis as the Leisure Centre and what have you? Without getting too hung up on buildings but in using the resources of the community. Among those resources were the schools and other things. Is it possible to make that easier? There are interesting places like Conway Mill, for instance, which is providing a function facility with a very interesting use of people and equipment, and the Flowerfield Centre. And particularly those places where there was a synergy coming from co-operative use and several different organisations and bodies. We saw a need for brokers. The brokerage role of, for instance, Workers' Education Authority.

We were anxious to give some emphasis to the value of theatre in education and the possibility of expanding that. There is a tremendous need for books as part of the resources, re-publication of books that had gone out, re-issue, the mere fact of being able to buy or borrow or get books. It might even be much more important to have a rack for paperbacks in a supermarket for instance than in some great building. Then, as I say, we talked of access through the schools and again the thought of education as a key centre. This permeated the whole discussion but there were structural difficulties. One of the structural difficulties people expressed actually throughout the morning, was what happened when you were forced to apply for package funding. You might not need much and either you fell or rose on that but the uncertainty that that produced inhibited development and growth. Another technical structural point was the difficulty created by things like having to get entertainment licences before you could go into schools or arts centres if you then wanted to charge admission.

There were some people who were deeply attracted to the idea of the Maison de la Culture. And then we went on to think of the people who were in these centres; the need for an animateur, but not lone rangers, people who are plugged into some system who could actually act as brokers, who could begin to bring people and resources together and enable things to happen, and the empowerment of those people by funds. The interesting thing again, and this is a point for the bureaucracy, people who are working in communities and working with groups were saying 'We don't want huge amounts of money, but we want it quickly but not a lot of strings'. £100.00 given in that sort of way can be much more valuable to them and the question was whether you could have some means of doing that which would bypass or short-circuit the bureaucracy. The importance of community arts, again we would want to stress that people are talking about the question of promotion and marketing, again one would see the animateur or the brokers in a sense doing that sort of thing as well.

We did not specifically address ourselves to the question of Irish and Irish music and what have you, simply because we thought that if we went to where people were, that was what you would take as a point of departure, what they had themselves. We saw no reason for treating Irish in any way different from the other. And we finished off, actually, with a great symbol which we want to sell you for the activity which we were about. It arose from Michael Longley's very powerful metaphor this morning, of people sitting on a gold mine with a toothpick. What we are asking you to do is to change the toothpick into a JCB and, if possible, a JCB GT.

SEMINAR DISCUSSION: THE ARTS

INTRODUCTION

The discussion converged around four themes. The first was concerned with identifying the most appropriate definition of the arts, and of culture; the second involved the particular character of existing cultural traditions, and the need to empower individuals and communities to explore and express their cultural inheritance; as a consequence, making the arts more accessible became the third topic; and lastly, issues were raised connected with the funding of the arts.

TOPICS

1. Definition of the arts.
2. Tradition as resource.
3. Access to the arts.
4. Funding.

1. Definition of the arts

The group was aware of the difficulty of defining the arts and wary of putting limits on them. The nature of artistic endeavour, inevitably an individual and slightly mysterious activity, requires a certain creative anarchy, and defies attempts to compartmentalize and make it manageable. Part of any definition should include the idea that art reaches past the rational and invokes the world of feelings and emotions. The arts as traditionally defined were regarded as too narrow; the arts may be interpreted as all creative activity, but increasingly, all intellectual activity directed at enhancing understanding of the life about us would be included. A 'soft' definition, the arts as solace for example, is to be avoided, and a more robust and challenging interpretation of the topic, incorporating social critique from, for example, sociological writings, was preferred.

Attention focussed on the relationship between the arts and culture, defined as everything human beings create. The arts were seen as a vehicle for the expression of culture, but which also transcend it and can cause it to take new directions; tradition is not immutable and a static, backward looking interpretation of culture is to be avoided. Although it was accepted that good art expresses universal truths about the human condition unconnected to place, it was felt that the immediate emphasis for Northern Ireland should be on facilitating the exploration of local identity; in this activity, art has a role in articulating and interpreting local experience and in enabling uncertainty to emerge.

2. Tradition as resource

The group expressed the view that local cultural traditions and assumptions need to be 'unpacked' to enable people to identify the elements which have meaning for them. This is particularly true for Protestant culture which has received little discussion or investigation and as a result is often assumed not to exist, although historically Protestants have been more productive in the arts, largely because of relatively advantageous social circumstances. Part of the reason may lie in the specifically religious dimension; religion is an important component in culture and a determinant of the way people look at certain aspects of experience. There was a perception that Protestantism does not value the arts in the same way as Catholicism and some forms of the religion may in fact be hostile to artistic and cultural expression. But there is imagery in the Protestant religion. There is also a vast, hidden Protestant culture, but a problem of secrecy exists which compounds the difficulty of investigating it. The tendency too for Protestant tradition to take a political form of expression hinders its sympathetic portrayal to outsiders. On an individual level the internalisation of political rhetoric may cause people to reject what is their own background.

There are thus areas of research which could usefully be done, particularly within the Protestant sub-culture. Nevertheless the prime need is to enable individuals to explore their own identity and determine their place within the group, even when some tension between the individual and the group emerges as a result. Exposing people to the arts may undermine secrecy through a process of discovery, and a lively artistic environment can enable people to review and reinterpret their own place in local culture and tradition. Making this sort of exploration possible requires permitting people to begin at the point they are at and to develop at their own pace. It demands the imaginative adapting of techniques to encourage participation initially, and subsequently to permit people to make their own contribution from the resources of talent and tradition latent in local communities, and to develop new directions. This will involve support for community arts, for art in education, for theatre-in-education, as well as providing access to the 'arts' in the more generally accepted sense. Broadening the horizons of young people by facilitating travel beyond the province would also be valuable. The aim is cultural literacy and the objective is to extend choice for people so that they are not locked in to a particular world view.

3. Access to the arts

The question then arises, how can people be encouraged to explore their identity in this way? The issue is at heart one of access. The type of structures which make it possible for people to unpack and share their background is not easy to determine. Both formal and informal educational approaches are important, the formal in terms of the need to press for full integration of the arts into the school curriculum, and the informal in terms of the need for continuing access to the arts through adult education. As a practical measure, school buildings could also be made available to arts groups; their use would help to overcome the artificial separation of education and the arts which works to the detriment of both. Making the arts more accessible is particularly directed at the economically marginalised, which is often associated with cultural marginalisation.

Arts centres have an important role but the nature of the role needs to be carefully worked out. If the result is to confine the arts within one building it will not improve access; an arts centre should rather be used as a resource and a facilitator. A parallel was drawn with the French Maisons de la Culture. Arts centres can be run by two or more agencies in co-operation, for example, district councils and the WEA, but the emphasis should be not on delivery of the arts to people but on getting people to participate.

The lack of access to appropriate literature was an area of concern. Both the north and south of Ireland are impoverished in terms of their own writings, largely due to dependence on British publishers. Much basic Irish literature can now only be found in rare bookshops. No other European country is so impoverished in this respect. Suggestions for the re-issuing of basic texts would include Estyn Evans; Lloyd Praeger; Carleton; and Protestant metrical hymns, psalms and sermons.

4. **Funding**

The feeling was widespread that the arts suffer from lack of resources; making them more accessible will inevitably involve increased expenditure. The small scale of many arts groups is an advantage in making them more accessible but can make them vulnerable to financial fluctuations. Only relatively small amounts of money are involved but sometimes need to be made available rapidly to avert a crisis. The capacity of the arts to generate in their turn employment and wealth is not paid sufficient regard when questions of funding arise.

Conclusion

In conclusion, the major agreed themes can be summed up as:

(i)   the need to free up local culture and traditions by revealing, through the arts, their dynamic nature;

(ii)   the need to empower individuals and communities to explore their identity and develop self-expression; and

(iii) the need to improve access to the arts.

Michael Longley's initial address to conference had included the metaphor of the goldmine to describe the potential for Northern Ireland of a rich diversity in its cultural inheritance. Without investment in resources for local artistic development however, the mining of that gold is being undertaken with a toothpick. The seminar group extended the metaphor by wanting to turn the toothpick into a JCB.

RECOMMENDATIONS: THE ARTS

In terms of funding the following areas demand attention, either through influencing the spending priorities of existing agencies or through separate funding:

(i)   creating properly resourced arts centres to act as focal points for the arts;

(ii)   republishing important works out of print;

(iii) allowing for small amounts of money to be made available quickly for arts groups;

(iv) publishing relevant research reports.

COMMUNICATIONS

Chairman: James Hawthorne

Former Controller, BBC Northern Ireland

Report to conference

We started off by looking at what might be called a matrix, an imaginary grid on a page with items along the top, other items down the side, and therefore points of intersection. At the top were all the normal definitions of communication; television and radio and press. Within television and radio sub-groups of news and current affairs, documentary and arts programmes and drama. And then publications, meaning the more informational, current affairs publications. We also have film and video noting that there is to be a huge structural change in the set-up both of the BBC and the ITV network. In the future 25% of BBC and ITV output has to be independently produced. Therefore there is an urgent need for the development of a new film and video activity. Video also includes the amateur who can now get excellent pictures with a camera costing £1,000 where a few years ago his camera might have cost £60,000. And there are other forms of communication. There is personal contact, there is tourism. We could have added to that top line. Then we thought of our targets on the side of our matrix. What are the targets? There are the decision makers, there are academics who have got to be engaged in the debate. There are the community groups and last and most importantly there is the general public.

Thus we had a fearsome amount of intersection points, and we could not deal with them all in detail. Symbolically perhaps, we discussed the BBC's *Talkback* programme on radio which seemed to demonstrate all the horrors and some of the possible strengths of popular media. A critical view was that such programmes fuel ill-considered and emotional debate. *Talkback* was seen as poison; too confrontational. The notion that too many programmes are confrontational had nodding approval in our group until we began to analyse the problem. Confrontation was defended and I think it was difficult to decide clearly as to whether confrontation is not an essential part of the debate, essential to democracy.

We noted research that showed that the media is not as brainwashing as we might think, that in the pre-school age groups youngsters' ideas are formed and that there is no strong evidence that fundamental beliefs and attitudes are later influenced by the media. Perhaps as representatives of the middle class we long for the days of John Simpson and Brian Garrett whose programme styles were less populist than the current *Talkback* but we recognised that effective broadcasts must appeal to large numbers. The phrase which in the end crystallised our thinking was that broadcasting should promote the 'integrity of dialogue'.

We could have talked until the cows came home about individual tastes in news and current affairs, about indigenous documentaries, and we would have expressed strong wishes about how the broadcasting institutions might promote cultural diversity. But we did realise that there is nothing we can do really about them. Media institutions will run their own affairs and the only course open to us is one of continual dialogue and persuasion. We would like to see more drama but we have to recognise that it costs £300,000 per hour. We did identify that there was possibly a need for training among journalists but even that point was contested when we noted that many who trained in Northern Ireland are holding senior positions in London.

We considered the possibility of manipulation. Should we as a pressure group attempt to manipulate the media, should we try to supply it with a particular range of material? Should we attempt to counter-balance confrontation and discord with harmony, with the good things in our Province? We decided in the end we were not the Tourist Board, a point which drew a cheer from a distinguished Tourist Board representative. Nor did we believe the media should be obsessed by 'balance'.

We noted a deterioration in our own provincial newspapers – what one press representative called the 'bingoisation' of the local press. Depressed by that evidence, we wondered if it would be possible to assist or subsidise publications at community level. But if so, what kind of publications would effectively carry material of cross-community value? We noted that we may be on the brink of a so-called desk-top revolution in publishing, and here we thought that some kind of subsidised training might be helpful.

But what is the cultural image that we wish to get across? There is much talk and concern about Ulster's image abroad and how we perceive our own image within Northern Ireland? Is our culture a compound of many influences fused into something unique? Or is it merely a mixture of separate disparate ingredients that suspend together as a mixture but which are not fused? Is this its strength? In the end we settled for the concept of a cultural heritage defined by Edna Longley: the North-East as a cultural corridor open at both ends.

We noted that between various cultural groupings there is growing dialogue and broader recognition of what culture can include. For instance, it is possible to speak of a 'flute band' culture. Whatever it is, it is the culture that produced James Galway. It has 'street credibility' and we noted that if our new cultural traditions campaign is to be effective, we too must have street credibility.

But what in the end were the seminar's recommendations?

With regard to the main media institutions – the press, radio and television – we must try to exert pressure where we can. In broadcasting it may be possible to subsidise certain kinds of programmes but, for various legal and 'constitutional' reasons the broadcasting organisations may have difficulty in accepting the sort of direct subsidy which would be seen as sponsoring. I believe that various forms of indirect help may be possible because more and more productions, especially in the cultural, documentary serious sector will be produced by independent companies. Quite apart from that, there is scope for greater co-ordination, which would not necessarily involve vast sums of money.

If, for example, the BBC's Educational Broadcasting Department is planning a particular series of programmes then other institutions should be aware of what is being planned. A museum might run a special exhibition; a publisher might see scope for producing a follow-up book. There might be an advertising campaign that would assist the plan as a whole. Subsidy could close some of the gaps and make a well co-ordinated, multi-media operation more cost effective. What is needed is a structure to enable museums, publishers, broadcasters, writers and educationalists to plan projects together.

We looked at film and video. These activities are developing fast at both professional and community level. We noted that the British Film Institute which stimulates activity all over Britain has no mandate for Northern Ireland – a scandalous state of affairs when one thinks what has been achieved in the training of film-makers in places such as the north-east of England. We see a real need for training in film and video in Northern Ireland, perhaps even in film journalism or even in simply encouraging young people to speak for themselves and to speak across to other communities through the making of films. Happily there is a structure in Northern Ireland on which we might be able to build – 'E Force'. There could be practical ways in which we could work out some assistance for that established group.

We noted too the experience of the Arts Council who have brought young people together for drama projects and the like. When the projects finish the participants are sadly deflated; they no longer have a reason for working together and consequently cross community achievement is dissipated. Young people are 'crying out' for projects to share. The seminar believed that the will to work together is there and what is perhaps needed may be some field workers to get more projects going. Here again it may not be necessary to start from scratch. The Northern Ireland Voluntary Trust has a long standing remit in this area and its work could be further subsidised.

In summary then: our seminar had a discursive start but we believe that for every door that is closed there are more that can be opened; that with more research and development of ideas it should be possible to draw up a number of strategies that really will make a difference to cross-community understanding. Put simply, we think it's possible to spread a little bit of happiness, a little bit of fun.

SEMINAR DISUSSION: COMMUNICATIONS

INTRODUCTION

The group was asked to consider communications with the aims of promoting a more constructive public debate on the different cultural traditions in Northern Ireland, and to challenge the conventional analysis of the subject.

The group was in general agreement that all of the communications media had an important role in helping us to learn more about one another by promoting constructive cross-community dialogue. It was suggested that one of the main themes of the discussion might be -

'A community in dialogue with itself'

In considering our cultural traditions many questions were posed. Can it be defined? What is it made up of? Is it plural/multi-cultural? Does it have a strongly Scottish element? Is it simply a mixture or could it be considered as a compound?

Following Edna Longley's metaphor, it was suggested that Northern Ireland can be best viewed as a cultural corridor in which there is a cross-fertilisation of traditions which are, and should be, celebrated. In presenting our cultural image abroad the intention should be to indicate the special nature of our pluralism. It was also felt that there was as much division within the traditions as between them and that there is work to be done in promoting internal dialogues.

Religion cannot be left out of the assessment of cultural image since it has a very important role in determining our perceptions of ourselves and others.

All topics were to be considered in terms of conventional communications and their potential targets. The conventional outputs were the broadcast media – television and radio; the printed media – the press and publications, and film. The potential targets ranged from academics and decision makers through to community groups and the general public.

The broadcast media included news and current affairs, documentaries and arts programmes. Publications encompassed periodicals, information leaflets, community pamphlets and informal publications as well as conventional publications. Film was particularly important in view of the future requirement for the broadcasting companies to use a substantial proportion of independent local productions. The group added contact, tourism and drama to the list of outputs and considered access to the young, particularly important.

In addition the group identified the issues of balance in media presentation, marketing as a means of improving the involvement in cultural events, and the influence of the media on the self-esteem of those working in cultural areas as worthy of inclusion in the discussion.

The discussions of the group are thus considered under the following topic headings which extend the set agenda.

TOPICS

1. Contact and Tourism
2. Broadcasting
3. Publications
4. Community Arts
5. Access, Support and Marketing.

1. Contact and Tourism

'Contact' was a very important aspect of communications and included music, sport, and even just talking, as for example at the John Hewitt summer schools.

Tourism related both to image and contact. There were two principle elements to this:

– encouraging as many visitors as possible to visit Northern Ireland to communicate that it is not quite as bad a place as it appears!
– permitting the 'locals' to see the view of outsiders (tourists) – often the value of what we have is not recognised until it is confirmed by outsiders.

In this context it was suggested that if local groups wished to put together a programme of events – cultural, musical, local history, then this could be given wide exposure abroad (given the great ease and speed with which FAX makes this possible) in the hope of attracting interested groups who might wish to take up such offers.

Within this context also, the value of making more of the Irish language was highlighted. It was suggested that Northern Ireland Tourist Board might include a publication in or about Irish as part of its general information pack. This would both be a useful way of giving the language recognition within Northern Ireland and of adding an element of 'mystique', often important in attracting outside visitors.

2. Broadcasting

a. Conflict/Confrontation in presentation

The view that there was too much confrontation at present within the media emerged immediately. The point was made with particular reference to the BBC radio programme *Talkback*. The group felt it was valuable to let the lengthy discussion continue as it brought out many general points.

The critical views centred on the programme's tendency to fuel conflict through reporting the basest elements of people's views. It was felt also that the anonymity offered by the phone-in format encouraged 'fireside bigotry'. The 'tabloid' content of the programme also came under attack as an unnecessary use of titillation to attract an audience.

The discussion addressed the important issue of whether the present action of real conflict and real (if unappealing) views had a place in the media. Despite the many criticisms, such programmes have an uncommon degree of community involvement – many people listen and are prepared to use it as a forum to express views which are not often represented in the media. However, it was suggested that rather than challenging views and positions *Talkback* often confirms prejudices because it is presented in a context too different from that of the listeners.

The critical views of the programme, initially described as 'that poisonous programme *Talkback*' were balanced by those who felt that there was, (and should be), room for a confrontational programme. However, although confrontation is an essential element of the presentation of programmes such as *Talkback*, there has been a tendency for this approach to spread into other broadcasting contexts. Those among the group who were frequent interviewees regarded the confrontational approach which forced them into the defensive position as unhelpful. Earlier programmes, such as those presented by John Simpson and Brian Garrett, had managed to deal with important issues in a journalistically sophisticated way, but had reached only a relatively small audience of the 'relatively converted'. *Talkback's* vernacular approach, has opened up a whole range of serious issues to a wide group within the community. It is perhaps unavoidable that 'quality' of presentation is traded off against breadth of appeal.

Generally it was felt that the media cannot shy away from confrontation in a community that is divided. Anything which provides a forum for dealing with conflict before it gets to the level of hand to hand fighting must be good.

b. Quality

The more general issue of the quality of the presentation/ interviewing in local broadcasting was taken further in discussion. Confrontation is a poor substitute for the technique of a skilled interviewer who, through key questions, explores crucial issues and it may be counter-productive, losing the goodwill of those being interviewed. Such confrontation may fuel conflict in the community.

There was some disagreement on the quality of local presentation of news and current affairs. One view suggested that Northern Ireland suffered more from the flying journalistic crews than from local journalistic effort which is more accountable and has more to gain from good production and presentation. Northern Ireland has also exported a great deal of talent to the national media.

The quality of indigenous documentary is high and the regional magazine programmes produced in the province are of a standard equalling, if not bettering, productions from other regions. However, it was felt that a lot of work needs to be done on training for current affairs programmes. Funding for training is required to allow those already working with video to acquire the skills to produce and present good current affairs programmes.

c. Anti-sectarianism

Another important issue which was raised, was the question of whether the media should simply be presenting material in a non-sectarian manner (as in the case of children's programmes) or whether it should present material in an anti-sectarian way. While there was some support for the latter position, caution was expressed from several perspectives. Firstly, despite widely held opinion, evidence suggests that the media are not actually capable of 'brain washing'. Information presented in a non- sectarian way may challenge accepted prejudices but may also, from the listener's point of view, be interpreted in a way that confirms prejudice. There is little evidence from research in the area of race and media that presenting an anti-sectarian view through the media can reverse prejudice.

Secondly, any attempt to present information in an anti-sectarian mode runs the risk of misinterpretation. If the media are seen to have an agenda then it is likely to lose its audience.

d. Drama

Drama has the potential both to affirm and be self-critical about cultural traditions and values. It is also valuable as a forum in which we can identify with those seen to be grappling with the conflict of our cultures. Drama, particularly on television, is very expensive, but offers a unique opportunity to present difficult issues clearly, in a context which is meaningful to the viewer/listener.

'Soap opera', while often not dramatic, was suggested as a very good medium for communication. It was thought that some consideration might be given to the development of a local 'soap opera' which could provide a forum for dealing with issues of cultural difference and conflict in a way which would reach a wide audience. It could deal realistically with the issues of every day life in Northern Ireland and provide insights into the alternative cultures which would challenge accepted views (something between *The McCooeys* and the *Billy* plays presented in the modern format of *Eastenders* or *Brookside*).

e. Training/development (What can be done?)

The broadcast media must, of necessity, present and deal with the conflict and confrontation which is inherent in our society and must do this in a way consistent with *promoting the integrity of dialogue within the community*

It was considered that there was room for improvement in the quality of local news and current affairs coverage, particularly in presentation, and that means of assisting the broadcasting institutions to maintain and improve standards should be sought. This might most appropriately be done through investment in training and development and the encouragement of quality independent and indigenous productions.

3. Publications

a. Books

There have been many noted achievements in local publishing over the last 20 years, but publishers feel they have been limited by the need to learn the profession, the development of a new and young local industry and financial problems. The industry has come a long way in overcoming the initial problems and is now well established. Books have a very important role to play in helping us to explain ourselves to one another but it is something of a chicken and egg situation. The industry needs to attract people's attention in order to fulfil this function and to become financially viable. But until it is financially viable it does not have the resources to put into promoting and developing publishing generally. Something very valuable could be achieved by channelling funding into the presentation and promotion of books, many of which would further the current aims of the Cultural Traditions Group.

b. Weekly/monthly publications

It was generally felt that people needed access to more well-informed current affairs publications but there were no suggestions coming forward on how this might be achieved.

c. Newspapers

A generally pessimistic view of the future of the local press was expressed based on the lack of investment of resources, the commercial interests of publishers and the increasing competition from national press (and radio and television).

It is likely that as circulation continues to fall we will see the treatment of politics and local current affairs increasingly trivialised in what should be a more reflective return.

There were no recommendations as to how this deterioration might be overcome.

d. Community newspapers

Somewhat counter to the pessimistic view expressed about the press in general, some people felt that the informal publications, which face the same problems of competing for the attention of a large group who do not have any great commitment to reading had succeeded in producing literature in a form that people will read.

There is, however, potential within the community and a great need to help people tell their stories. It may be worthwhile to help groups to exploit the new technology of desk-top publishing thus making professional and attractive presentation a possibility for community groups.

The possibility of exploiting the already extant free sheets which have an enormous circulation as a means of accessing large numbers of people was mentioned. The problem is how to avoid the danger of exploitation by those with the greatest finance/influence. There was also the further danger that an expansion of community newsheets through access to desk-top publishing could lead to an increase in sectarianism.

4. Community Arts

The Arts Council should continue to support activities in the community that are generative of art/culture or affect the nature of expressive art in the community. The aim should be to build a solid cultural base for expressive art in the community, without which the 'higher level' forms of art cannot develop (James Galway and the flute band culture cited).

Further sponsorship of activities, such as those promoted by the Arts Council in which groups of children work together creatively (which differs from the general run of the mill sporting activities etc which are essentially competitive), would be welcomed by the group.

The group expressed support for the many activities which are already serving a very important function of building cross-cultural contact and communication at all levels. The practicalities of achieving these aims fell into the following areas:

5. Access, support and marketing

a. Access to key target groups

The key target group was thought to be young people. It was suggested that the assembled 'old crumblies' were perhaps not capable of fully appreciating the most important medium to get across a message to this group. For the young, pop culture is likely to be more important than 'cultural traditions'.

The even younger group should not be overlooked. It is clear that children's perceptions are often formed before going to school and ways of accessing this group must be identified. The pre-school era and pre-school materials need to be part of the cultural traditions agenda.

These age-related access problems are compounded by the increasing incidence of teenage parents raising pre-school children in a working class environment. There are few opportunities within the current format of the conventional media to reach these groups. The most appropriate medium/media to bridge the gaps of age, social class and cultural diversity must be considered.

A further 'access' problem was how to help people to find out about what is going on in the community. Advertising might help those who already had potential projects.

There was general support for the idea of supporting those with skills in the community to enable them to become facilitators who could help people formulate and carry through projects. The model of the Northern Ireland Voluntary Trust was one which was suggested as a potential means of providing an effective groundwork structure in the community.

b. Marketing

There is a general difficulty in publicising what is already happening in many areas.

It would be necessary to look at the needs and resources appropriate to enable cultural events to be covered by the media in a co-ordinated and high profile way.

The profile of events could be raised with effective marketing, which might involve subsidised advertising. The group was in general agreement that there was value to be derived from passive contact with events in addition to that derived from active participation, and that this should be exploited. Many more people hear about what is happening than get the opportunity to participate. The value of this passive contact is that it forces the listener/viewer to take a view on events/issues even though they may not actively participate.

c. Self-esteem

The role of the communications media in reinforcing value and raising self-esteem was echoed by many of those present. Giving events a higher media profile reinforces the value of the work very many people are doing in small groups and serves to raise their self-esteem.

The best can often be brought out in people if they are given just a little bit of praise: one of our local failings is that we do not give sufficient recognition to the valuable work which goes on in the community. If an effective way could be found for the media to do this regularly, and in a relatively high-profile way, this would be of enormous value.

Principles and proposals

Following their wide-ranging discussion, the group endorsed a number of general principles and made some specific recommendations: The group endorsed the following principles:

i. within the cultural image of Northern Ireland there is a pluralism which should be celebrated through the cross-fertilisation of traditions;

ii. all branches of the communications media have a very important role to play promoting goodwill and mutual understanding throughout the community;

iii. the media also play a valuable role in reinforcing value and self-esteem throughout the community;

iv. broadcasting in particular has a responsibility to 'promote the integrity of dialogue within the community';

v. the media should not be expected nor pressurised to present an unrealistic balanced view. The challenge is for the media to present views of the alternative traditions, with greater insight, but without being obsessed with balance;

vi. what is done or attempted through the current exercise must have 'street credibility'. It must be seen to be of and for the people and not generated through a process of 'cultural imperialism';

vii. the value of building a solid culture base by focussing on things which are both supportive and generative of art/culture within the community.

RECOMMENDATIONS: COMMUNICATIONS

The following positive action was recommended:

1. Tourism

i. further steps should be considered to encourage as many visitors as possible to Northern Ireland, particularly through greater development of attractions for special interest visitors;

ii. the Northern Ireland Tourist Board should promote broad packages/programmes of events put together by local groups which attract special interest groups;

iii. the Northern Ireland Tourist Board should consider the possibility of including a publication in or about the Irish language in its general information pack about Northern Ireland.

2. Broadcasting, television and radio

iv. we should assist the broadcasting institutions, where possible, to raise the standard of news and current affairs coverage in Northern Ireland;

v. there is a need to develop serious commentary on current affairs;

vi. the nature and quality of journalistic training in the Province needs consideration;

vii. the production of quality independent indigenous documentaries should be encouraged;

viii. consideration should be given to building on the already high quality local broadcast drama as a means of promoting constructive dialogue within the community;

ix. the possibility of improving RTE reception throughout Northern Ireland should be explored as a means of broadening horizons and allowing people to see a different view of themselves and others.

3. Publications

x. funding should be provided to develop the presentation and promotion of books and publications on local topics;

xi. funding should be provided to make the facilities of desk-top publishing available to local community groups;

4. The Arts

xii. subsidy should be considered to develop effective marketing of cultural events.

xiii. the Arts Council should promote and support events/ activities that are generative of expressive art/culture in the community.

Priorities

To address the issue of priority the group considered the practical implications of these recommendations. The suggestions needed to be tied down to an administrative system that would allow the building from the bottom up, bearing in mind that the exercise must have 'street credibility' and be prepared to speak in many voices.

It was suggested that, in the context of the present exercise, priorities might best be established by identifying those areas that are most susceptible to influence by money. Three principle areas were identified:

1. Broadcasting/Film making – the need for investment in the training of broadcasters and film makers. There is the possibility also of providing pump-priming subsidy for local productions. (It was noted with dismay that the British Film Institute does not operate in Northern Ireland and there is no similar source of support or funding for independent film makers).

2. Increased support for publishing – to include a shift of emphasis to a wider range of published materials than the Arts Council would normally be concerned with and able to fund.

3. Sponsorship of community based activities which are supportive or generative of expressive art/culture. This might involve the development of a network of ground-level facilitators, drawing on skills already extant, who would work within the community to promote and develop untapped potential.

LOCAL STUDIES

Chairman: Brian Turner

Curator, Down Museum

Report to conference

The seminar group on 'Local Studies' may have felt some disappointment that the subject was actually categorised into a separate group because we all felt that the place of local studies must be affirmed as central to all the concerns of this conference. I heard quite a few echoes of our discussion in what Maurice Hayes has said, although generally speaking I don't think I've heard as many as I was expecting from the other groups.

The upsurge of interest in local studies is a fact, although it is sometimes unrecognised. We want to assert it and deal with it. In relation to the specific concerns of this conference we felt that those concerned with local studies would be cautious of large scale oversimplifications. We would assert that local studies can individualise and humanise perceptions which are much more readily caricatured on a larger scale. At a local level, rather than a simple two way division, harsh as we know it is in some areas of life, we are much more likely to recognise a tapestry of Presbyterians and Roman Catholics and Methodists, urban folk and rural folk, mountain folk and lowland folk and wealthy people and poor people, and O'Neills and Thompsons and Hollywoods and Greenaways, and Cafollas. What I am saying is that local studies would be concerned to challenge the use of the 'two traditions' terminology. We are alarmed that, because of the fact that some parts of life in Ulster demonstrate a clear two-way difference of opinion, this simple division is presently being pushed into areas where it is inappropriate and unhelpful. As an influential group of people (as I was told we were when I got my letter like the rest of you) those concerned with promoting a pluralist society must stop reinforcing the rigid notion of 'two traditions'.

As regards 'the sense of place', it is much easier to accept than it is to keep redefining it. We largely did accept the vital importance of the notion of place, in the healthy sense of Patrick Kavanagh's definition of 'parochial', which can mean confidence and universality, as opposed to the 'provincial' which always looks over its shoulder at what someone else is doing.

Although we did recognise the rise of interest in local studies, there was also reference to ways in which our sense of place may be seen to be breaking down, as illustrated in our attitude to our environment. Our attitude to our built environment is generally disgraceful, and the problem of litter all over the place was mentioned with feeling.

Another aspect which was discussed, and may at first sight seem minor but is actually deeply significant, is what is happening to our place names. One of the most destructive factors as far as the sense of place is concerned is the relatively recent post office system of rural road naming which is destroying the use and the knowledge of our townland names. John Campbell last night demonstrated that our townlands are a vital part of our sense of place and a building block for the identity of Ulster people, urban and rural. It must surely mean something profound, when we look hard at ourselves, to observe local authorities supporting the invention of Gaelic street names in towns, and at the same time conniving at the destruction of the genuine and ancient Gaelic names of the countryside. It often makes me think that many of the alleged representatives of 'Gaelic' tradition wouldn't know an Irish dimension if it bit their nose off.

With regard to local museums and local studies we did want to point out the simple statistic that local historical societies in Ulster have increased in number by fifteen or twentyfold in the last generation. This increase is certainly something significant particularly in view of the fact that it has coincided with a period of social unrest. With regard to Ulster society in general, I think that a gathering such as this must always bear in mind that the vast majority of the community about whom we are talking would feel very uncomfortable if they were here with us now. I did note Maurice Hayes saying several times that we must start where people are – and that is one of the strengths of local studies.

Those of you who know me know that I am fairly simple-minded, and our group did actually come up with a list of things which might be done, as I thought we were requested to do.

Firstly, we felt it essential that a conference like this should not simply be about money. I have heard it said several times that it may have been unhelpful to mention that a million pounds was available for 'cultural traditions' before this conference rather than after it. One thing that should come out of this conference is a determination to set up a steering group to work out a framework which will discipline the distribution of any available money. We do not want to get into the situation of the lottery-led culture in the Republic where, because of the presence of money, people are furiously thinking up projects which will get some of it. We want to be much more disciplined than that. So that was one recommendation – that this conference gives rise to some sort of discipline and policy – not simply invitations for people to ask for money.

With regard to local studies in particular we felt that, because of the nature of the interest, a certificated course in methods of local study would be valuable. This is not to be confused with teaching the history of localities, but should be a course in methodology for people who do not necessarily have any formal qualifications. This should be provided by a third level institution and, without making any more specific remark, we wanted to commend the work and the potential of the Institute of Irish Studies at Queen's University.

Some of you may know that the Federation for Ulster Local Studies draws together the local historical societies of Ulster. It has associated with it the Ulster Local History Trust Fund, with trustees which include some people here and others like Seamus Heaney, M B McGrady, and Lord O'Neill. Our group recommend that this Fund be endowed sufficiently to staff and maintain an office which will co-ordinate local historical and environmental work as it relates to the voluntary movement. We do not want it to concern itself only with the voluntary movement, but with those things that are relevant to the voluntary movement.

We also recognised and affirmed the relevance of a dedicated strand of local studies broadcasting, and we hope it will continue to develop.

We did not want simply to make a list of the many people who were terribly worthy, but we were minded to say that there should be increased support for the Linen Hall Library.

Local museums figure particularly in our discussion of relevant types of institution which are not yet fully established in Northern Ireland. What we mean by this is that national museums are fully established, even though they might like more money, and likewise the BBC and UTV are 'established', but local museums do not yet have a clear profile. By 'local' in this case we mean roughly 'county'.

Local museums should be properly structured and resourced, and we should not fall into the position which exists in Britain where there are hundreds of small museums and many of them are helpless.

And finally, getting back to place names – there is little more evocative than place names. We want to express the extraordinary grievance which is felt through large areas of the country at the destruction of our townland names. Representation should be made to the Post Office and local authorities to stop this, which is one of the greatest twentieth century acts of vandalism against the sense of place in Ulster.

As I am the last in this series of reporters from the seminar groups I think I will leave you with a quotation. I was not intending to do so, but I want to return to the idea that there are a lot of people out there who are not able to articulate their feelings, but that does not mean they are not to be regarded. They are indeed the important people. We referred in our seminar to two small farmers who refused to knock down their traditional Ulster gate posts because their machinery was too wide to go through them. Instead they got three car jacks and moved them out wider and put them down again. That kind of attitude needs to be recognised and respected, and not patronised. So although none of us can express our deepest feelings I would like to give you a quotation on this area of thought from John Montague, or Montaig, as he might be referred to at the grass roots. I leave it with you as an expression of something in which I think we all ought to know we are involved.

> The whole landscape a manuscript
> We had lost the skill to read,
> A part of our past disinherited;
> But fumbled, like a blind man,
> Along the fingertips of instinct.*

NOTE

*John Montague *The rough field* 4th edition, Portlaoise, 1984.

SEMINAR DISCUSSION: LOCAL STUDIES

INTRODUCTION

The Local Studies Seminar Group noted the aim of the conference which was to engender constructive public debate on how diverse traditions can be affirmed and enjoyed in a manner which is not threatening or divisive and the particular remit of their group to make positive proposals which would contribute to the development of policy. They also noted that they had been asked to challenge the conventional analysis of the subject. In his introduction the Chairman indicated that there may not be a conventional view of local studies but it was necessary to reassert that the subject had wider relevance and importance than simply as an antiquarian hobby. Indeed it was essential to affirm the place of local studies as central in any celebration of diverse traditions. The local studies perspective, focusing initially on where people were, dealt with the building blocks of identity and provided an avenue to greater awareness and understanding of people's current position. The Chairman then referred to the four topics that the seminar group specifically had been asked to consider.

TOPICS

1. The variety of influences on our identity.
2. The role of established organisations.
3. The sense of place.
4. The role of local museums.

1. The variety of influences on our identity

There was recognition and acceptance by the group that there were a variety of influences on our identity. Indeed there was a strong feeling, given a concern with pluralism, that it was important to avoid reinforcing the rigid notion of two communities where the only split of significance was in terms of religion. There was a need to reassert the importance of uncovering the complex confusing truth rather than accepting a categorisation based solely on terms of two traditions. Whilst local studies were important in themselves, they also had a central role to play in the context of affirming the value of diverse traditions. Through a focus on locale it offered people the opportunity to start from where they were, and to examine how, in terms meaningful to them, the variety of influences on their identity had been formed. Through better understanding of their local situation at a time when the increasing scale at which society operated exerted strong countervailing forces there was potential to understand better the wider situation. At the same time, however, there was a need to recognise the concomitant danger that in being seen to advocate local studies as a cure for society's ills the subject could lose its spontaneity and enthusiasm and risk being discredited.

2. The role of established organisations

There was considerable discussion of what more established organisations could do to aid the development of local studies. Publication and assisting publication was noted as a crucial area whether it was small books for children or easy to read material for adults. Aids to local study were also considered important – how to go about finding out what is available in your local area and having someone to help. In this context there was discussion of how longer opening hours, for example at the Public Record Office, might assist. Discussion on this topic graduated to the need to develop the skills of those interested in local study on how best to go about the task. Members felt that there was a need to develop a certificated course on methods of local study at a third level institution but it was important to ensure that entrance to such a course was not conditional on applicants having formal qualifications. Members noted the previous lack of success in interesting the various institutions in the need for such a course, but it was suggested that a fresh approach might meet with a more receptive response.

At the same time it was pointed out that major strides had been taken in the last number of years in the development of local studies. There had been a spontaneous growth in the number of local history societies from three in 1960, nine in 1970, forty-four in 1980 to over sixty in 1988. Allied to this, resource based learning had been carried further in Northern Ireland than in many other places with some innovative members of the teaching profession making a substantial contribution.

3. Sense of place

The Chairman questioned whether there were things that showed that our sense of place is breaking down. Whilst on the one hand the increase in the number of local history groups in the province testified to an increased sense of place and pride in place there was still evidence of a disregard of place ranging from the amount of litter in our environment to institutional insensitivity of the kind exemplified by the Post Office exclusion of townland names from the postal address system. Members agreed that there should be more scope for inherent pride in locality to find expression. It was essential to recognise the importance of, and not to patronise, examples such as that given by two County Down small farmers who faced, with the need to widen their gates to facilitate the passage of modern farm machinery physically moved their traditional stone gate posts rather than knocking them down, as is now customary.

It was considered that there was an important role for the Federation for Ulster Local Studies in ensuring that voluntary bodies with an interest in conserving those things in our heritage that are good and worth keeping came together with one voice. Groups interested in natural as well as human history should also be recognised. Highlighting a sense of place and the preservation of its positive aspects and the encouragement of community interest and involvement with such issues could have a valuable community development role.

In the context of a sense of place specific mention was made of the loss of townland names in the postal address system. This meant de facto that they disappeared from the minds and lips of the people and there was a strong feeling that the issue should not be allowed to rest. It appeared worth exploring whether the need for a unique identifier in the postal address system could exist alongside the townland nomenclature.

4. The role of local museums

The importance of properly constituted, financed and resourced local museums in developing local studies was referred to. If the value of the subject was accepted it must be backed up with adequate funding. Local museums acted as an important point of contact for the community in developing a sense of place and were active vibrant institutions involved in all manner of innovative activities contributing much to general community development. Often they pointed to what was good in the preservation of the architectural heritage and showed what could be done in terms of conserving buildings of note. However having access to adequate financial resources especially on the current expenditure side was a continuing problem. Here too members felt there were parallels with the work of the Linen Hall Library, uniquely situated in the centre of Belfast, where it was felt particularly unfortunate that staff had to spend such a considerable amount of time in fund raising rather than developing the role of the library. All this pointed to a need to examine priorities in terms of fostering awareness of cultural diversity.

RECOMMENDATIONS: LOCAL STUDIES

In the light of their discussion which affirmed the importance of local studies in fostering knowledge and enjoyment of diverse cultural traditions the group made the following recommendations:-

(i) There is a need to set up a central steering group to decide policy prior to the disbursement of any public funds aimed at facilitating development. This would provide the necessary framework and discipline for the allocation of money to the many groups involved in increasing appreciation of diverse traditions;

(ii) A certificated course in *methods* of local study and research on place should be set up. It should be located at a third level institution but acceptance on the course should not necessarily be confined to those with formal qualifications. In discussion of this topic the group noted the valuable work and important role of the Institute of Irish Studies at Queen's University;

(iii) The Ulster Local History Trust Fund should be endowed sufficiently to staff and maintain an office to develop and co-ordinate the work of the Federation for Local Studies in its interface with the large voluntary movement;

(iv) The group encourages and affirms the relevance of a dedicated strand of local studies broadcasting. Current media recognition of the importance of local studies was welcomed and a proposed series of local studies programmes on Radio Ulster was noted;

(v) A limited number of securely based local museums have enormous and varied potential in helping the community to know itself; they should be adequately structured and financed in terms of both capital expenditure and recurrent costs;

(vi) Reference was made to the need to provide sufficient funding to the Linen Hall Library such that it could continue its work free from continual financial threat;

(vii) The extraordinary grievance of the loss of rural townland names is an issue which should not be allowed to rest and fresh representations should be made to the Post Office and others on it.

OPEN FORUM

The Chairman asked for comments

Belinda Loftus: Arts Officer, Down Council

One point that was referred to in the Arts Seminar was slightly at a tangent, but it was very strongly felt. This was the fact that the Home Secretary's recent edict on the appearance on television of people from particular groups, or people who were seen to be supporting particular groups, is actually editing out whole areas of history, let alone current affairs. For example, I have been informed that Robert Kee's excellent series, *Ireland, A History* could no longer be shown under this edict.

Clem McCartney: Centre for Conflict Studies, University of Ulster

First of all, the point which has just been made by Belinda Loftus, about the problems caused by the media ban on representatives of groups like Sinn Fein and the Ulster Defence Association, was also mentioned in the media and communications group. But I also wanted to say that, as I listened to Maurice Hayes' report from his group, I was very struck by the similarity between his comments and a theme which came through again and again in the media and communications group. This was the importance of relating to people's current situation, and building culture from people's existing culture, and the resulting need for animateurs to assist with this process.

Charles Fitzgerald: Belfast Newsletter

I recently wrote in *The News Letter,* about why Protestant Ulster appears to have rejected the harp and it got one of the biggest mail bags I've experienced. Many readers wrote claiming that they just didn't want to know. The harp, they said, had nothing to do with them, in effect claiming that the harp had been taken away from the crown, that it had no longer anything to do with them. It was no longer their harp even if ever it had been their harp. I had asked 'where was the pride in the harp under the crown?' 'Where was our pride in being Irish in an English society?' Those are I think, questions we (and Protestant Ulster) are going to have to address.

There is another basic problem and I think it is this: there is a refusal to accept that ULSTER exists. Whether as a province, whether as part of the Irish entity, or as part of the British entity. Whether as a part of Europe or a part of the rest of the world. There is a general reluctance to accept that we have progressed to the stage that the place damn well does exist. And all the traditions, all the history, or anything else will not eliminate that fact at this moment.

Protestant Ulster itself is searching, desperately searching, for an identity. Protestant Ulster is searching for an identity rejecting the harp, because it believes that same harp, long the symbol of both Ireland and Britain and of Ireland within a British society, no longer belongs to it nor has any relevance to it.

I speak of Protestant Ulster with a small p, perhaps I should speak of Calvinist protestant Ulster? Conversely, is Protestant Ulster seeking for something which is not there? Has it an identity? Has it had an identity? Will it find an identity? Is it today, and now, doing or trying to do, what the Gaelic element did at the end of the last and the beginning of this century? Is it trying to create a new identity that will fit its present and prove acceptable to the current state of things? Is it trying to replace one identity (presently perceived as unsuitable) with another that seems more suitable at the present time?

These are matters which must concern us, concerning as they do our heritage or our various heritages. They are matters which should concern everyone on this island, North or South, for neither history nor heritage can afford to be misinterpreted, appropriated, or misappropriated by any sector or section. Heritage can (and often is) perceived in different ways by different people. Indeed, there are those who will (and do) try to twist heritage to suit their own perceptions and beliefs.

If this conference, representing as it does a very broad cross-section of Northern Ireland, can make an attempt to define heritage or heritages, then what transpires at this conference should be known by everyone, not just those who are partaking in it. People must know what heritage, and whose heritage before they can share and understand heritage be it a common heritage of different heritages. Which is why I, for one, believe that if this conference is to be worthwhile, the debate and the contributions and the evaluations should reach as wide an audience as possible.

Colm Cavanagh: NORIBIC, Derry

I would really like to make two points: one is very much in the spirit of the local studies theme that we have heard about. I know that even though I studied history right through college and in my first year at university, it was only when I came back home I started to discover what the history of my own town was. It reminded me of a lovely metaphor of standing in a large room, in total darkness and not knowing how large the room was – until slowly people began to switch on the lights of local history and I began to understand the size and shape and dimensions of the room; who else was in the room; and how important it was. What we have since done in Derry is to found what became the Guildhall Press. Using Action for Community Employment funding which is readily available from Government, and with the sympathy and encouragement of the Community Projects Branch of the Department of Economic Development, we have already published about a dozen booklets on various aspects of life in Derry in particular and the North West in general; Hiring Fairs; the history of the Shirt Industry; the Bridges and River Ferries; Derry Jails; biographies of local people etc etc. (We subsequently got a new manager for the project who decided that there was enough of this educational stuff which people didn't want to read. So he began to publish quiz books and joke books and the sales went up enormously!)

The second thing I wanted to say was that I am pleased no one has worried out loud over the last 24 hours about the 'watering-down of traditions', because there is a tendency when we come together at a time like this for people to declare that we must preserve the integrity of everything we grew up with. I for one would like to put on record that I am quite happy to water down some of my traditions. And I wish some other people would be a little bit prepared to water down theirs as well. Having said that, and I am going to be one of the last speakers from the floor, could I just say that I'm very pleased that I came. I found this a very interesting and stimulating twenty-four hours and I will certainly go away with a good few ideas either refreshed, reinforced or maybe implanted in my mind for the first time about things that I personally will be able to do. And I don't have to leave it to the Department of Education, or the Cultural Traditions Group, or the Government, or various other groups within the community. There are a whole lot of things that I can do either better than before or maybe start afresh; and I would like to thank the Cultural Traditions Group for giving me that opportunity.

Tom Hadden: Queen's University, Belfast

How does one join the Cultural Traditions Group. The point has been made that there is a danger of a relatively small group of people taking the thing over: I think that some effort should be made to open it up, let other people join.

James Hawthorne: Chairman, Cultural Traditions Group

This is not, I hope, a reply churlish to Professor Tom Hadden's kindly inquiry about membership. It's something I did want to say anyway; a brief word of explanation about the Cultural Traditions Group.

We're still toying with its very name and indeed we had been meeting for many weeks without having any name whatsoever. In fact, when we were inviting Roy Foster to come here we were unable to give a name to indicate who exactly we might be. That remains a problem!

We are certainly not an academy of elected members but rather a group which came together somewhat haphazardly, a group of fairly busy people, and we've simply been trying to identify, and talk through, a series of problems and find a few answers to some of them. We haven't been able to set a time scale though ultimately we want to assist, perhaps after a long struggle, in the development of new, and possibly long overdue, official policies. Whatever the present temporary structure of the group might be, it will change and grow. Nothing is as yet defined. But I know that those people who presently make up the group will be grateful for help and involvement from all, or any, of those here present.

Nor is it our intention, clearly, to reinvent the cultural wheel or to become an impressive quango. But what this conference has brought home is this: there is great wealth in our own culture and it is ready to be tapped and developed. The task for all of us will be to increase that wealth and to reinvest it in our own community. A possible priority is to think first of the younger sector of the community.

So may I say three things. First thank you for giving up the time. You might all have been watching the international rugby match at Murrayfield on television. But you have chosen to be here to apply your minds to the solution of serious problems. What has started as a 'cultural traditions' group is, as a group, going I know not where. But however things develop, collectively you have made a marvellous contribution toward achieving change in present thinking and policies. My thanks therefore to you.

And on behalf of you, I should like to thank the American Ireland Fund for its grant of money which made this meeting possible.

And third and finally, I'm sure you would all wish to join me in thanking George Quigley for his splendid, stylish leadership, direction and chairmanship of this very significant conference.

CONCLUSION

Conference chairman

We have come to the end of what I think has been an enjoyable and fruitful conference. To have managed to turn that tooth pick into a JCB in the course of twenty-four hours is no small achievement but I think we have probably done that. I shall not even attempt a comprehensive summing up, since the proceedings are fresh in our minds and there will be a published version to provide a convenient aide- memoire. But I would like to round off with a few concluding observations.

I think there are very few people who will have made remarks that have been agreed by the whole assembly but I feel that there is one remark made by David Trimble, repeating what was in the literature of the conference, around which we could all coalesce and that is the statement that our aim quite simply is to see how diverse traditions can be affirmed and enjoyed. Another vital idea permeating all our proceedings was the need to have a concept of cultural traditions which is as inclusive as people's perceptions of those traditions, and also the need to connect with the community at large for maximum impact. I think there will also be general agreement that no-one is talking about infiltrating one tradition by stealth into the camp of another. What we are talking about is providing opportunities for knowledge, tolerance, and mutual understanding to develop. Finally, we are not necessarily talking about taking ambitiously massive strides all at once but, equally, no-one wants to stay on the static exercise bicycle for too long. Let us not defer doing anything until we can do everything which ideally might be done. That was the sense, certainly, which I got coming from the conference.

Another point which has emerged clearly for me is the sheer volume of material about our cultural traditions which is now available. Obviously that will keep expanding in the future as well. I personally think that it is virtually impossible to keep track of it all, still less to absorb it so as to ensure that it is as widely disseminated as it needs to be. Valiant efforts are being made to achieve more co-ordination and cohesion but I wonder whether a great deal more does not need to be done to bring together what exists in a form which can be assimilated by a great many more people than are involved at the moment. You could think of a number of possible homes for a project of that kind, which could well be a joint venture funded from some of the new resources which the Minister has just announced for cultural traditions work.

I also wonder whether we do not need to reinforce greatly, perhaps at selected points throughout the province's library service, the books and pamphlets and reviews which are available to the public so that a good deal of the standard core material is readily accessible. Those sub-regional cultural sections could be linked with local museums and history societies and plugged into the central academic and cultural support facilities in the Province to form an original network for cultural traditions activities through the schools and other bodies. All that links up with Maurice Hayes' point about local arts centres and about the need for animateurs but not lone rangers to promote and back up such activities. I think it also links up with what Brian Turner was saying about the desirability of a course in methods of local study, which also could be a valuable addition. And when we are talking about the possibility of new networks or new arrangements, that, as Maurice Hayes said, need not necessarily entail bricks and mortar. I think we also want to underline the need to exploit to the full the potential of what we already have. In other words we need to influence the spending priorities of the existing agencies.

The education service is rightly regarded as an indispensable vehicle for purposes of what Sean Fulton described as 'acculturation', and there are many examples of what is already being done and many more suggestions today for more that might be done in the future. Accepting fully all the time-tabling difficulties, I wonder whether it may not be necessary to give cultural traditions a higher profile and to find ways of making it a prestige subject which attracts the commitment of the brightest pupils? There is plenty of scope for inter-school collaboration on cultural studies work, with exchanges of teachers and joint projects.

And I wonder whether the ramifications of our subject do not lead, perhaps, to a need to re-examine how we organise in schools the study of all the topics involved. Is there a case for a comprehensive programme which illustrates all the acts and artifacts of our cultural traditions, some of which are currently dispersed over a whole range of educational programmes?

We also need to be thinking – and this was a point several seminar chairmen made – about the adult population, and perhaps particularly but not exclusively about people who have left school in the last twenty years or so. What role have a whole series of organisations, with which men and women in this range might be involved, to play in the work?

The press, radio and television are, of course, key players in this age range and for the population at large – and crucially, I think, and this is a simple point, in arousing sheer interest: indifference (studied or casual) to cultural traditions alien to those which we perceive as our own can breed unnecessary insensitivity to matters which are of crucial significance to others. One difficulty is that so much of the media's material, into which a great deal of time and effort is put, proves ephemeral. There must be a whole mass of material in the archives of all these bodies which is worth making available in more permanent and subsidised form to encourage wide distribution. What, for example, about a quarterly, local Listener-type magazine (and I do not mean in precisely that form) which would reproduce in appropriately edited form some of what we have missed, or hear and too quickly forget? I will take two examples. What about the magnificent W. R. Rodgers 1949 interviews with those who knew Yeats, which was repeated on radio a couple of weeks ago, or last weekend's programme on the Drennan letters?

A great deal was said today about locality and place and I recalled some words of Seamus Heaney which I jotted down and which seemed to me to speak in a very lyrical fashion about the interaction of past and present within the context of a local space.

> That timescale, that double sense of great closeness and great distance subtly called into question the factional and sectarian closenesses and distances which have been pervasive in that part of the country. I do not say that a sense of the mesolithic ancestor could solve the political problems of the Bann Valley, but I do say that it could widen and clarify the lens through which we inspect the question of who we think we are. . . .. The gazer (at the artifacts of the past) is . . . transported for a moment into a redemptive mood of openness and readiness.[1]

The contributions on the arts, in what was said by James Hawthorne and Maurice Hayes were extremely interesting. I think we might recall in this context some words that were written by Louis

MacNeice many years ago that are still relevant. He said that the writer should be not so much the mouthpiece of a community (for he will only tell it what it knows already) as its conscience, its critical faculty, its generous instinct. Heaney himself writing many years later refined that in a very interesting way when he spoke of the tongue of the artist unconstrained 'by considerations of tact and fidelity, by nice obeisances to one's origin within the minority or the majority'. The idea of the freedom of the artist working within the community in that way is an extremely challenging one.

There was some very useful discussion of the Irish language, and some proposals. I think perhaps we also were reminded in the seminar activity of what is being made accessible by translation. Reference might also be made to the mode of translation which is, Heaney has said, trying 'to carry the tone of Irish across the linguistic divide'. He describes as having 'subtly to do with the deepest value system that the group speaking the language is possessed by'.[2] Brian Friel's translation of Chekhov, from existing English translations, is in effect seeking an identifiable new language. He believes that 'once the voice is found in literature . . . it can move out and become part of the common currency'.[3] One gets a sense of the tremendous variety within the English language which can reflect a variety of traditions.

Could I now come briefly to just a few concluding general observations, perhaps to bring our minds back to some of the general themes that underly all that we have been doing.

I suggest first of all that the conference has recognised that our cultural traditions are closely bound up with our whole symbol and image system, its conscious articulations and its hidden underpinnings. Our community, like other communities, has to confront in a responsible way what the sociologist would call the management of meaning. That requires tolerance, bred of knowledge and comprehension – and patience, because we should be wary of making any easy elision between knowledge and comprehension, still less between comprehension and tolerance.

It is tempting to view the present in Northern Ireland as a variant on the cyclical themes of hope, despair and apathy which some have discerned in Irish history generally, and there is obviously a sense in which, to use John Montague's phrase, we see 'a dark permanence of ancient forms'. Even if the hatchet is buried, few forget where they buried it. There is also the contrary temptation to dissolve the past 'in a kind of retroactive vague commonality' (a phrase of Fritz Stern in the context of German history), 'giving oneself the history that sets one free of history', as Hans Blumenberg has it, and then to indulge in facile extrapolation to a benign future.

One detects in modern debate on Irish affairs a disposition to transcend both temptations. It is acknowledged that retrieval of ancestry is a necessary means of avoiding intellectual amputation and that the past should be used for the interrogation rather than the reinforcement or deconstruction of myth.

One also detects a recognition in recent years that language has a most unfortunate habit of turning life into problems in the name of understanding. There is therefore less cultural narcissism now in Irish studies throughout the island, less desire to define and label the self or even the group in terms of a rediscovered past, less preoccupation with the search for the 'essence' whatever that may be. There is a learning from the scientist that (as Stephen Jay Gould has it) it is often a mistake to seek the 'essence' in a single criterion with an identifiable point of emergence. The 'essence' may have its origin in separate components and the focus should then be on the modes of their amalgamation. That augurs well, of course, for pluralism, because it may lead, in time, to the spelling out of a larger part of existence in the cultural alphabet of community rather than of group.

One might change the metaphor. Those engaged in cultural studies have, I suggest, embarked on a voyage of discovery, which may be also a voyage of self discovery. Some at least believe that this generation may be better to bend its energies to making landfall, leaving it to the future to invent a cosmology to accommodate the new world, whatever that may be.

In introducing Roy Foster yesterday, I referred to the risk of tradition subverting history, bringing 'history to a standstill', to borrow Richard Kearney's words, and making us 'contemporaries with the dead generations of the past'.[4] We therefore need to distinguish, I suggest, between – the tradita which are handed down and may vary from age to age – and traditio the living process of tradition. This living tradition (again to reflect Kearney) may degenerate into a mere object of idolatry, 'excluding dialogue with all that is other than (itself)'. Or it may serve as 'creative symbol'.

The notion of tradition serving as creative symbol is, I think, vital. As Joseph Brodsky has said, a ruin is a rather stubborn architectural style (not least, one might add, in Ireland) and one would like to think that dreams of tomorrow would exert at least as strong a pull in

Northern Ireland as visions of yesterday. Professor Lee has identified, for the South, the interdependence of historical perspective,
cultural change and economic development, and he has urged the
need to work very hard at forging the type of mentalité essential to
sustain long term collective achievement.[5] I believe that his point
has equal application for Northern Ireland and that learning to
handle our cultural traditions so that they serve as creative symbol is
vital for the future well being of our entire community.

Most communities represent opposing vested interests in temporary equilibrium. Realism therefore suggests that some friction is
inevitable. Indeed, in moderation, friction, rather than bland consensus, may be a necessary condition for progress and creativity.
However, if I might adapt V. S. Pritchett's words, the existence of
opposed interests should not prevent the crossing and re-crossing
freely of the frontiers which are constituted by the cultural rifts and
seams of the community. I hope you will agree that this crossing and
re-crossing has been a most successful feature of our Conference and
augurs well for the future.

In conclusion, I should like to congratulate once again the Cultural Traditions Group on its initiative and most important of all, to
wish it well on your behalf, as it seeks to carry these matters forward.

NOTES

1. S. Heaney, *The sense of the past*. Lecture given to the Friends of Monaghan County
   Museum 1984. Reproduced in *Ulster Local Studies* (Vol 9, No. 20, 1985).
2. S. Heaney, *The government of the tongue* (Faber and Faber, 1988).
3. Brian Friel *Ulf Dandanus* (Faber and Faber, 1988).
4. Richard Kearney, *Myth and Motherland* in *Ireland's Field Day* (Hutchinson, 1985).
5. Joseph Lee, Whither Ireland: The Next Twenty-five Years in *Ireland in Transition*,
   ed. K. A. Kennedy, (Mercier Press, 1986).

BIOGRAPHIES

Dr James Hawthorne
Former Controller, BBC Northern Ireland and Director of Television and Broadcasting, Hong Kong.

Dr George Quigley
Former Permanent Secretary of the Departments of Manpower Services, Commerce and Finance. Honorary Professorial Fellow of Queen's University, Belfast.

Dr Roy Foster
Professor in Modern History, University of London. Author of *Charles Stewart Parnell* (1976), *Lord Randolph Churchill* (1981) and *Modern Ireland 1600–1972(1988)*. Holder of British Academy Research Readership to work on authorized biography of W. B. Yeats.

Mr Michael Longley
Arts Director, Arts Council of Northern Ireland. Leading poet and Fellow of the Royal Society of Literature.

Mr Jack Magee
Formerly Principal Lecturer in History at St Joseph's College of Education. Honorary Fellow of the Institute of Irish Studies, Queen's University, Belfast.

Mr Christopher Napier
Practising solicitor and Chairman of the Northern Ireland Committee of the European Bureau for Lesser European Languages.

Mr David Trimble
Senior Lecturer in the Faculty of Law, Queen's University, Belfast. Chairman of the Ulster Society.

Professor Sean Fulton
Director of School of Education and Pro-Vice Chancellor, Queen's University, Belfast.

Professor David Harkness
Professor of Irish History, Queen's University, Belfast.

Dr Maurice Hayes
Formerly Permanent Secretary of the Department of Health and Social Services and Chairman of the Community Relations Commission. Presently Ombudsman, Honorary Senior Fellow, Institute of Irish Studies, Queen's University, Belfast, and Honorary Professor of Social Policy and Administration, University of Ulster.

Dr Brian Turner
Curator of Down Museum, Downpatrick, and Secretary of the Federation of Ulster Local Studies.

Acknowledgments

Thanks are due to the trustees of the John Luke estate for permission to use our cover illustration. We gratefully acknowledge the assistance of Professor E. Estyn Evans in allowing us to use his drawings. For permission to use 'Cultra Manor' by John Hewitt, published by Blackstaff Press and an extract from 'A Sense of the Past' by Seamus Heaney in the journal of the Ulster Federation of Local Studies, we thank the publishers.

POSTSCRIPT

Three months after the Cultural Traditions conference we can look back on an enjoyable, stimulating and influential event. But we can do more than that: we can report progress.

Drawing on views expressed during the conference, the Group has brought to Government new thinking on objectives and priorities of a £1 million per year cultural traditions programme involving schools, the arts, the museums and local cultural and heritage activities. We have also addressed the specific issue of the Irish language.

But perhaps the most important step has been the emergence of a Community Relations council, which will combine the responsibility of developing cultural diversity with the task of supporting cross-community activity at other levels and in other ways. In the coming months help is to be given to a range of projects which will contribute both to cultural development and to community relations.

Much, therefore, is owed to the participants at the conference, whose insights, goodwill and candour will have helped us all to look afresh at our own corner of Ireland, to test our strengths and to assert our unique blend of history, imagination and thought.

JAMES HAWTHORNE